A Guide to Parliamentary Papers

By the same authors:

Hansard's Catalogue and Breviate of Parliamentary Papers, 1696–1834
Select List of British Parliamentary Papers, 1833–1899
A Breviate of Parliamentary Papers, 1900–1916
A Breviate of Parliamentary Papers, 1917–1939
A Breviate of Parliamentary Papers, 1940–1954
Luke Graves Hansard's Diary, 1814–1841

With Diana Marshallsay:

Select List of British Parliamentary Papers, 1955–1964

By P. Ford:

The Economics of Collective Bargaining
Social Theory and Social Practice

SOUTHAMPTON UNIVERSITY STUDIES IN
PARLIAMENTARY PAPERS

A Guide to Parliamentary Papers

What They Are
How to Find Them
How to Use Them

Third Edition

P. FORD and G. FORD
University of Southampton

ROWMAN AND LITTLEFIELD
Totowa, New Jersey
1972

First edition, Oxford 1955
New edition, Oxford 1956

Third edition © 1972 Irish University Press

First published in the United States 1972
by Rowman and Littlefield, Totowa, New Jersey

ISBN 0–87471–100–2

All forms of micro-publishing
© *Irish University Microforms   Shannon   Ireland*

FILMSET AND PRINTED IN THE REPUBLIC OF IRELAND AT SHANNON
BY ROBERT HOGG PRINTER TO IRISH UNIVERSITY PRESS

To Eleanor and John

CONTENTS

PART I

WHAT THEY ARE

PART II

HOW TO FIND THEM

Contents
•

PART III

HOW TO USE THEM

Contents

APPENDICES

BIBLIOGRAPHICAL AIDS

PREFACE TO THE SECOND EDITION

This Guide has been written to assist students, researchers and those interested in public affairs who want to consult or read parliamentary papers. It has arisen out of many years spent in guiding such readers, and the information it contains has all of it at some time or other been given in response to their questions. Since our aim has been to assist those whose main interest is in the contents of the papers to understand and make effective use of them, we have avoided dwelling on any details of parliamentary procedure unnecessary for this purpose; these can be found in the standard books.

Two notes have been added which may be of interest to scholars. In one we have endeavoured to clear up certain obscurities in the history of the various collections of parliamentary papers and to make intelligible the numerous and varied sets of indexes issued in the first half of the nineteenth century. In the other we have traced the development of certain characteristics of the form and content of Hansard's *Debates* which affect their standing as historical evidence.

We have to thank Mr J. H. Hansard for permission to use certain extracts from L. G. Hansard's unpublished diaries which bear on the formation of collections of papers and their indexes, and Mr David Holland, Assistant Librarian of the House of Commons, for allowing us to check our detailed list of alphabetical indexes with his, and for help in connection with problems relating to the Third Series, known in the House as 'the Green Set'. Our thanks are also due to H.M.S.O. for its continued help.

We have taken the opportunity given by this edition to add brief notes on the publications of nationalized industries, on Lords' papers before the nineteenth century in the House of Lords Record Office and on the location of the bound sessional sets.

PREFACE TO THE THIRD EDITION

In this edition of the Guide several revisions and additions have been made to take account of the changes in the form and availability of the papers. There have been developments in the types of bodies making investigations or issuing papers and an increase in the number and proportion of policy papers published as non-parliamentary papers and therefore not in the sessional sets and indexes. We have elaborated a little on the way the papers came to Parliament, and have added from *Luke Graves Hansard's Diary* some further information on the printing of Command papers through the departments. To make it more convenient for users we have rearranged the material on citations, collections and guides, etc., into a single section on bibliographical aids.

We have refrained from going too deeply into the historical details as our main aim is to familiarize the researchers with the different kinds of papers, to explain the apparatus for finding them and to indicate the most profitable way of extracting information from them.

We offer our most grateful thanks to Miss D. Marshallsay for the meticulous care with which she went through the second and the draft of this edition, and also for compiling the index.

PART I

What They Are

The term 'parliamentary papers' is sometimes used broadly to cover everything officially published which concerns Parliament and its work, from the record of its proceedings and debates, the reports of its own committees and of outside bodies on public affairs to documents officially issued by departments in connection with their routine business. However wide the subject or specifically technical in detail, each paper or group of papers forms a part of a discernible pattern of activity and shows some facet of Parliament's work and thought. But it also has a narrower and more precise meaning, referring only to particular groups of papers coming before either House and included in one of its numbered series. The popular term, 'blue book', used to refer to these 'sessional' papers, arose in the nineteenth century when the printer used a blue cover on most of them, especially the larger ones, though many had buff covers, and some no covers at all. A 'white paper' is thus a blue book without a blue cover, but the term is also used with an additional meaning to refer to a particular kind of paper, such as a short statement on Government policy of the kind we have been so familiar with since 1945.

The 'green paper' developed in 1967 from the 'white paper' in that the proposals it contains are tentative and circulated for consideration. Such proposals may later be issued in a final form. Under the influence of the modern sales technique there is an increasing tendency to vary the colour and design of papers, so that the colour of the cover will have no specific meaning, though the short term, blue book, may remain in common usage.

The best method of classifying parliamentary papers must depend on the questions asked about them. Students of procedure and officers of the House or of Her Majesty's Stationery Office will naturally want to know the source from which they are derived and by what authority they are prepared, printed and presented or not presented, to Parliament. Sir T. Erskine May's discussion of them in *Parliamentary Practice* and Lord Campion's in *An Introduction to the Procedure of the House of Commons* are naturally written from an 'inside the House' point of view. They draw attention particularly to the origins of the papers, and the terms used to describe them are those familiar to the officers of the House and are significant to the student as he becomes acquainted with its procedure. But students of public affairs or history may be more interested in the contents of the various papers and the way in which they may be found than in the detailed processes and authority by which

1

they are issued. From this point of view the following groups can be distinguished:

I. Papers relating to the agenda, proceedings and debates of the House.
II. Papers giving Parliament information and other material bearing on questions of policy, administration and other matters which it may have to consider.

Papers in the second group may be said to come from two different sources:

a. House papers. These arise inside the House itself in the form of the reports of its own select committees, or as a result of its own request for or insistence upon being given information, such as reports it has specifically called for or has required by statute.
b. Others arise outside the House, that is, from the activities of Royal Commissions or Government Departments. Some of these, whether reports of inquiries, statements, or annual reports, may be brought to the notice of Parliament by being 'presented' to it as Command papers. Others may be published with the authority of the departments and not formally presented to Parliament.

House and Command papers, together with bills, form the sessional papers, i.e. parliamentary papers in the narrower sense already mentioned.

The distinction between these three groups—House papers, those arising outside and 'presented' and those arising outside and not 'presented'—is an important one, not only because of the different procedure by which they come into being, but because the arrangement of the papers and the steps which must be taken to find them are affected.

I. Papers Relating to the Agenda, Proceedings and Debates of the House

(a) *Procedure Papers*

In order to organize its complicated business thoroughly, Parliament of necessity provides its members with an elaborate and comprehensive series of procedure papers in the form of minutes, agenda papers, notice papers, etc. Some of these are of ephemeral interest only, while others are of more importance as a source upon which other and more valuable records are based. The *blue paper* is of the latter kind. It deals with the daily proceedings of Parliament, the most important items being: (1) the Votes and Proceedings of the previous sitting; (2) notices given at the previous sitting of questions, motions and amendments for future sittings; (3) the agenda for the day; (4) the proceedings of recent sittings of standing committees; (5) collected and marshalled lists of amendments to be proposed to bills soon to be considered; (6) division lists.[1] The first group, Votes and Proceedings, is a record of all that was, or was deemed to be done by the House on the previous day. It ignores everything that is *said,* unless it is specially ordered to be entered. In 1680 the Votes and Proceedings were ordered to be printed, and until 1742 they were the only record of the proceedings authorized by the House.[2] The entries are compiled on the responsibility of the Clerk of the House by the Votes and Proceedings Office, mainly from the entries in the minute books of the clerks at the Table, and are printed and circulated to members on the authority of the Speaker. It also gives the minutes of proceedings of the standing committees, which include the results of divisions and the names of members voting in these committees. On the other hand, the *white paper (notice paper)* which contains certain portions of the blue paper and relates to the current day's sittings, and the *order book,* which is available each day and shows the programme, so far as modified, of the future business of the session, are of the former group.

(b)   *The Journals*[3]

The Journal is the official record of the proceedings of the House, compiled each day in the Journal Office from Votes and Proceedings and the minute books of the clerks at the Table and is used by the officers of the House, whose reference book it is for those precedents of the House required by the Speaker when ruling on points of order. The first Journal, known as the Seymour Journal, was written in 1547 by a clerk of the House. In 1742 the Journals were ordered to be printed, and by 1761 the printing was brought up to date. In 1803 the House made an order for reprinting, and by 1825 they had been reprinted up to the fifty-eighth volume. The Journal is not drawn up in the form of minutes, but in a more explanatory narrative form and a continuity of style has been preserved since the seventeenth century. It thus records very fully and formally a number of things which used to be done and are still supposed to be done, but which are very properly now taken for granted, that is to say, the form has survived the fact, so that on matters of precedent it is an unsafe guide to anyone not familiar with its conventional language.[4] But it is the most accessible record of the activities of Parliament for over four centuries and is therefore a mine of information invaluable to scholars.

1   Strathearn Gordon, *Our Parliament*, 6th ed. (London 1964).
2   H. Hale Bellot, 'Parliamentary Printing, 1660–1837', *Institute of Historical Research Bulletin,* XI (1933–34), 87.
3   See memo by the librarian on 'Printing of the Journals of the House of Commons' in *Publications and Debates*, Sel. Cttee. Rep.; 1914–16 (321) iv.
4   See evidence. qq. 520–63, by Sir Courtenay Ilbert: *Official Publications,* Sel. Cttee.; 1906 (279) xi.

3

(c)   *The Debates (Hansard)*

The Debates are the official records of things *said* in Parliament. They are substantially verbatim and in the first person. From 1803 to 1909 some speeches were given in full, the rest being abbreviated accounts, and the record was a mixture of the first and third person. Originally the Debates were published as a private venture by William Cobbett. They were designed to form a continuation of *The Parliamentary History from 1066 to 1803,* of which volumes 1 to 12 are entitled *Cobbett's Parliamentary History* and volumes 13 to 36 *Parliamentary History.* At different times there had already been published many separate series of histories either of Parliament, the proceedings of Parliament, or the debates of Parliament, from 'original sources',[5] and these were used by Cobbett and later by T. C. Hansard to do what he described as 'completely superseding' other collections.[6]

Thomas Curson Hansard, who was printer for the first volume of the History (1806) and the tenth volume of the Debates (1808), took over both projects after Cobbett sold out his interests in them in 1812. In the Advertisement in the 1813 volume of each series Thomas Curson Hansard announced that they were 'published under the superintendence of T. C. Hansard', and from 1829 he printed on the title page of the Debates *Hansard's Parliamentary Debates.* They became commonly— and since 1943 officially—known as *Hansard.* Two generations—Thomas Curson Hansard, senior (1776–1833), eldest son of Luke Hansard, Printer to the House of Commons, and Thomas Curson Hansard, junior (1813–91)—conducted the enterprise, later with the help of a government subsidy, until the latter sold out his interest in 1889. The House of Commons had decided not to continue to subsidize the Debates but to put them out to contract under the supervision of H. M. Stationery Office. In 1909 these arrangements were terminated when the House of Commons appointed its own reporting staff and H. M. Stationery Office did the printing.

(d)   *Standing Committee Debates*

Standing committees representative of the whole House are appointed each session to deal with various classes of Public Bills after the second reading. 'All standing committees have leave to print and circulate with the Votes the minutes of their proceedings and any amended clauses of bills committed to them. The minutes are printed and circulated after each sitting of a committee and at the conclusion of the consideration of each bill are reported to the House by whose order they are reprinted

5   A note on the methods of compilation, accuracy, style and length of the debates is given in Appendix II.
6   See *A Bibliography of Parliamentary Debates of Great Britain,* House of Commons Library, Document no. 2 (H.M.S.O. 1956).

and published as a parliamentary paper.'[7] A shorthand note is taken of the debates in standing committees by the official reporters. It is usual to publish an official report of the debates on a Government bill, but in the case of a private member's bill, a report is published only when the chairman of the committee considers that it is required in the public interest.

II. Papers Giving Parliament Information for Consideration

(a) *House of Commons Papers*

These are the papers which arise out of the deliberations or are needed for the work of the House and are 'Ordered by the House of Commons to be printed'.[8] The first order to print is recorded in the Commons Journal in 1641, and although from that date the papers have been affected by changes in Parliament's methods of acquiring them and in the scope of its work, the feature which distinguishes them is the 'order to print'. They consist of the following groups:

> Bills
> Reports of Committees of the House
> Returns
> Act Papers

(i) *Bills.* Bills are of two classes—public bills and private bills. The former relate to matters of public policy and are introduced directly by members of the House. The latter are bills for the particular interest of individuals, public bodies or local authorities, and are solicited by the interested parties. Bills are printed on their introduction into either House and are usually reprinted with the amendments made during the course of their passage through Parliament, Commons bills being arranged and numbered as a separate series. Public and General bills are printed by the Queen's Printer; bills dealing with private or local interests are printed by the promoters and not officially printed until they have received Royal Assent as Acts.

(ii) *Reports of Committees.* Committees of the whole House,[9] i.e. the whole House sitting as a committee, arose in the seventeenth century during the period of the struggle between Crown and Commons. It was

---

7 Thomas Erskine May, *Parliamentary Practice,* 18th ed. (London 1971), pp. 598–615.
8 For some years before 1835 a number of reports of Royal Commissions bear the same legend. See p. 25.
9 J. H. Willcox, 'Some Aspects of the Early History of Committees of the Whole House', *Parliamentary Affairs,* VII, no. 4 (1954), p. 409. Gilbert F. M. Campion, *Introduction to the Procedure of the House of Commons,* 2nd ed. (London 1947), pp. 25–29.

a device to allow for an informal discussion on a particular issue; the mace is taken from the Table, a chairman appointed to take the place of the Speaker and the rules of procedure relaxed. It was also used for inquiry, e.g. hearing evidence on petitions relating to interruptions to trade during the Napoleonic Wars as a result of the Orders in Council,[10] and in a quite different field, evidence on a bill to disfranchise East Retford and to enable Birmingham to elect two representatives instead. Today this form of committee is not used for inquiry, but only for deliberation.

As the name implies, *select committees* are not committees of the whole House, but consist of members of the House of Commons (or the House of Lords) chosen as representative of the parties and shades of opinion of the House. A Joint Select Committee consists of members of both Houses. Each session a number of select committees, known as 'sessional committees', are appointed to deal with matters of a particular class arising during the course of a session; of these, the Select Committee of Privileges and that on House of Commons (Services) are examples. There are two select committees on financial matters, the Public Accounts Committee, whose primary function is to ensure after audit that money has been spent as Parliament intended, and the Estimates Committee.[11] The latter reviews departmental estimates and of recent years its reports often contain valuable information not found elsewhere. The *Select List of British Parliamentary Papers, 1955–1964* (p. 103) gives a list of Estimates Committee reports during these years. The rest are appointed to deal with particular subjects as they arise and make reports by the end of the session, but if a committee has not finished its work by then, it may present any material it has collected, such as minutes of evidence, and advise the House to re-appoint a committee in the following session to complete it.

Before, and well into the nineteenth century the select committee was the chief means by which Parliament conducted its investigations. This is seen by an examination of the (alphabetical) *Index to Reports from Select Committees, 1801–1845*. The select committee is still an important investigating instrument of Parliament, though as the nineteenth century progressed more and more of the work of investigation was undertaken by the Royal Commissions and Departmental Committees. But since 1955 there has been some renewed use of this form of inquiry. As the activities and powers of government departments increased, proposals were canvassed from time to time to appoint standing committees of the House to take an interest in their activities. These ideas received general approval by the Haldane Committee on the *Machinery*

10   *Orders in Council,* Mins. of ev.; 1812 (210) iii.
11   Replaced by Expenditure Committee, 1970–71.

of Government (1918).[12] In practice not much came of this until after 1954, when the successive select committees on the nationalized industries set to work. Then, following an announcement by the Leader of the House, Mr Crossman, in December 1966 during a debate on procedure, there were appointed two select committees on 'departments' —one on Agriculture which made four major reports and was then disbanded and one on Education and Science—and several on 'subjects' —Science and Technology, Race Relations and Immigration, Scottish Affairs and Overseas Aid.

The reports of select committees have special features which arise from the fact that they are reports of committees to the House which appointed them. They therefore contain (1) the report on the subject referred to them; (2) a record of the proceedings of the committee day by day, which normally includes the text of any draft report submitted by the chairman, together with any amendments proposed, and a record of the voting; (3) the minutes of evidence, if any, taken by the committee. The House is then fully informed of what took place in the committee and the record of proceedings is sometimes a valuable guide to the trends of opinion in the committee. In this respect those documents differ from the reports of departmental committees, referred to later, which do not report proceedings and need not publish the evidence taken.

(iii) *Returns*. 'Return' is a term used inside the House for those papers Parliament requires from the departments in the course of its work. When calling for these papers the House uses an historical formula which it faithfully observes. Papers other than those on financial matters required from those departments which grew out of the Royal Household, e.g. the Treasury and the Home Office, are called for 'By Humble Address to the Crown'. But when information is wanted from those departments created by statute, such as the Local Government Board, it is called for 'By order of the House'. This method of extracting information was used considerably in the nineteenth century, both as a means of pressure from Parliament to get information from ministers, particularly on foreign affairs,[13] and for obtaining reports from what in fact were departmental committees. The appearance of an increasing number of committee, as distinct from select committee, reports as House papers, indicated Parliament had asked for them as returns and Parliament had ordered them to be printed. These reports are distinguished by the legend they bear, for example, *Return: Mercantile Steam Navy* is the title printed on the cover; on the title page it is 'Return

---

12   Pp. 14–15; 1918 Cd.9230, xii.
13   Harold W. V. Temperley and Lillian M. Penson, *A Century of Diplomatic Blue Books, 1814–1914* (Cambridge 1938).

to an order . . . Copy of a Report of the Committee appointed by the Board of Ordnance to inquire into the Capabilities of the Mercantile Steam Navy for Purposes of War'.[14] The *Committee on Legal Business of the Government*[15] was called a departmental committee, but its report became a 'return' to an order and is a House paper. The use of the 'order' became of less relative importance as departments thought it necessary to present their printed reports, or as more papers came to the House automatically through a statutory requirement. The following is an example of the kind of information which Parliament might require at any time. It arose out of a public discussion on the alleged forcible feeding of a suffragette: 'Return to an address of the Honourable the House of Commons for Correspondence of the Home Office with the Royal College of Surgeons and Sir Victor Horsley with regard to the case of Lilian Lenton'.[16] Though it is now rare to call for a paper, it is 'open to a Minister himself to put forward a motion calling for Papers and this constitutes a useful means whereby certain statistical returns are laid before Parliament. Thus the monthly Trade and Navigation accounts used to be presented by the Board of Trade as a Return to an Order[17] . . . and the Annual Statement on Experiments on Living Animals is presented by the Home Office as a Return to an Address'.[18] In this way the term 'return' is kept in current use and is usually understood to refer to papers of a statistical nature.

(iv)   *Act Papers.* The 'act papers' are those which an Act of Parliament has required should be laid before the House and which it has ordered to be printed. Nowadays the order to print is given only for the more important of them. Examples of such papers are the annual reports of the Gas Council, the National Coal Board, the Atomic Energy Authority and the New Towns Corporations. An examination of any recent sessional index of House papers 'By Act' will show that many of them are financial reports and accounts.

(b)   *Papers Arising Outside the House*

These are first, the reports and papers of Royal Commissions, which are appointed by Royal Warrant. The second group consists of departmental papers, i.e. those issued on the authority of a government department. They include the reports of committees set up by departments and of departmental officers, State Papers on foreign affairs, annual reports of ad hoc bodies, statistical returns, etc.

14   1852–53 (687) lxi.
15   1877 (199) xxvii.
16   1913 (190) lii.
17   Trade and navigation accounts are now called Overseas Trade Statistics and are non-parliamentary.
18   H.M. Treasury, *Official Publications* (H.M.S.O. 1958), p. 8.

Royal Commissions[19] and departmental committees or other investigating bodies report to their appointing authority, that is, to the Crown or the Minister, and not to the House. Their reports and papers can be brought to the notice of the House by being presented to it 'By Command'. Command papers differ from House papers because of the constitutional form[20] that instead of being 'Ordered by the House of Commons to be printed' they are (technically) 'Presented by Command' of the Crown.[21] That the reports of Royal Commissions will be presented by Command is obvious. Some of the departmental reports and papers are also presented by Command, but others are not and are issued on the direct authority of the department and not through the House. Thus there are reports of committees set up by departments which are presented, and reports which are not. It is therefore convenient to begin by thinking of the various types of investigating bodies and of the different kinds of papers arising outside the House—both those of Royal Commissions and departmental papers—whether they are presented or not.

(i) *Reports of Royal Commissions.* The Royal Commission of inquiry consists, in constitutional form, of a body of persons appointed by the Crown to inquire into the subjects named in the Royal Warrant.[22] In fact, of course, the persons appointed and the terms of reference are the

19 Royal Commissions of inquiry should be distinguished from administrative commissions or commissioners which may be established by statute to perform particular tasks and may be required to present reports to Parliament, e.g. Ninth Report of the Commissioners for the *Exhibition of 1851;* 1934–35 Cmd.4895, viii; *Boundary Commission (England and Wales),* Report, etc.; 1917–18 Cd.8756, xiii.

20 For the form observed in presenting papers, see May, *Parliamentary Practice,* pp. 251–2.

21 The annual estimates are an exception. 'They are Presented to the House of Commons By Command, but the voting of Supply is so essentially a House of Commons matter that they are given a House of Commons and not a Command number and are printed on the authority of the House.' H.M. Treasury, *Official Publications* (H.M.S.O. 1958), p. 9.

22 Royal Commissions were the earliest ad hoc bodies appointed by the Crown for investigatory purposes, and were sometimes used in the sixteenth and seventeenth centuries for the investigation of social problems and as a preparation for legislation, for example, the Commission for Inclosures, 1517. But the reports were not laid before Parliament even when they had been set up in response to petitions from it. After 1660 Commissions fell largely into disuse owing to the bad reputation which certain administrative commissions had acquired under the early Stuarts, and their place as instruments for government inquiries was taken in the latter part of the seventeenth and the eighteenth century by select committees of either House. Such commissions as there were during this period were chiefly administrative in character and reported to Parliament under the terms of acts which created them. H. S. Cobb, 'Memo. No. 20' (typescript) House of Lords Record Office, 1959. *Guide to House of Lords Papers and Petitions.*

result of ministerial advice. Unlike the select committee, which is composed entirely of Members of Parliament, and whose life does not exceed one session, unless re-appointed, and whose findings are printed by order of the House, a Royal Commission may be composed of people whom the Minister considers to be experts in the subject to be investigated, or of experience in public affairs generally, and who need not necessarily be and mostly are not Members of Parliament. Further, where the time is needed to finish an investigation, a commission's inquiries may last over a number of years. Another advantage over a select committee is that it need not stop its work when Parliament is not sitting, and if need be it can send all or some of its members abroad to take evidence. For example, the Royal Commission on the Natural Resources, Trade and Legislation of Certain Portions of His Majesty's Dominions, 1912–18, sent some of the members to take evidence in Australia, New Zealand, South Africa and Canada. For these reasons it has proved to be a more high-powered, as well as a more flexible, instrument of investigation than the select committee.[23] Normally, the commissions report within two or three years, though some may sit for four or five. Occasionally a commission of inquiry may have a special task or develop a special task, and what began as a commission of inquiry becomes, in fact, a permanent body. One example is the Royal Commission on Historical Manuscripts, which now publishes periodical or annual reports.

(ii) *Departmental Papers.* As Parliament extended its supervision over the economic and social life of the country, the work of existing departments grew, new departments were created and there was a corresponding development of new forms of investigating committees sponsored by the departments themselves. These include departmental committees, advisory and consultative committees and working parties. Unlike select committees but like Royal Commissions, these committees may or may not include Members of Parliament, and they may extend their inquiries over a considerable time and outlast any given Parliament. They report not to the Crown or to Parliament, but to the Minister. Unlike a select committee or a Royal Commission, reports from them may or may not include any evidence they have taken—in these days very often they do not. Nor do they include any record of proceedings, as does a report of a select committee. If a searcher wishes to find out what went on in a committee the document, other than in Reservations or Minority reports, will tell him little or nothing.

---

23   For lists of royal commissions in the nineteenth century see Hugh M. Clokie and J. William Robinson, *Royal Commissions of Inquiry* (Stanford 1937). For the twentieth century see David E. Butler and Jennie Freeman, *British Political Facts, 1900–1967,* 2nd ed. (London 1968), pp. 175–79.

Departmental Committees. The description of 'returns', already given, makes it plain that reports, first of 'committees' and then of 'departmental committees', as distinct from select committees, appear first as House papers and then as Command papers. This indicated that the Minister was using a more elastic method for investigating problems, especially those of purely departmental origin, and that he did not have to set in motion the historical paraphernalia which surrounded the setting up of a Royal Commission. In fact, just as the Royal Commission had taken the place of the select committee, so the departmental committee replaced or shared with the Royal Commission the work of major investigations.

Advisory and Consultative Committees. The advisory committee is mainly a departmental invention, though some have been created by statute. Examples, like that on *Commercial Intelligence* set up in 1900, are to be found in the early part of the century, but work of the Ministry of Reconstruction during the First World War gave this form of committee an impetus, and this was added to by the recommendation of the Haldane Committee on the *Machinery of Government* that departments should make fuller and more frequent use of them.[24] In general, their members are persons of special knowledge, and such a committee provides a minister with a body of experts to whom he can refer problems in a particular field of his department's work as they arise. He is saved the trouble of finding the experts he needs for a particular investigation, and he can establish a continuity of expert knowledge and experience and thereby anticipate the problems of his department before they become matters of public policy in Parliament. Or they may provide him with expert assistance in the administration of Acts of Parliament. That their terms of reference often take the form not of 'to inquire into' but 'to consider and advise' is itself significant of their character and function. Thus, the Salisbury Advisory Panel on Housing was asked to report on the emergency housing problem at the close of the First World War, and the Women's Housing Sub-Committee played a considerable part in the discussion on housing standards and requirements. In the light of later problems of hospital organization under the National Health Service, the report of the Consultative Council on the *Future Provision of Medical and Allied Services* of 1920 is a notable document.[25] The outstanding example is the Consultative Committee of the Ministry (Board) of Education, set up in 1900 by statute, with the provision that not less than two-thirds of its members were to be persons qualified to represent universities and other bodies interested in education. The

24   Pars. 34–37; 1918 Cd.9230, xii. See also *Poor Laws,* R. Com., Minority rep. p. 1209; 1909 Cd.4499, xxxvii.
25   1920 Cmd.693, xvii.

influence it has exerted on educational policy and administration through its long series of reports, such as the Hadow Report on the *Primary School*[26] and the Spens Report on *Secondary Education*,[27] needs only to be mentioned. After the Education Act, 1944, the active bodies were the Advisory Councils set up under section 4 of the statute with the specific duty not only of advising the Minister on questions he referred to them, but also on such matters connected with the theory and practice of education as they thought fit. The Crowther Report on *15 to 18*[28] and the Newsom Report on *Half Our Future*[29] are notable examples of their work. In contrast to the nineteenth century, when the great reports on education were those of Royal Commissions, in the twentieth century they have been rather those of the Consultative Committee and Advisory Councils. The advisory body has become one of the chief media for keeping ministers in touch with outside opinion. Many departments now have a number of advisory committees or councils, sometimes very large in membership and composed of specialists and people knowledgeable on matters within their fields of responsibility.

Working Parties. 'Working party' is a military term, the use of which spread during the Second World War from the Services to other government departments as a name for small groups and committees charged with the investigation of some problem or the preparation of some scheme. As the name implies, a working party was usually small, less formal in its proceedings, and its members were expected to take an active part in the work. Working parties therefore shed some of the paraphernalia of committee procedure in much the same way as the departmental committee shed that of the Royal Commission. Quite apart from the fact that during and immediately after the war everybody was so busily occupied that the time-consuming process of formal hearings of evidence was not always practicable—the suspensions and difficulties referred to in some of the reports of committees issued during 1915–19 exemplified this—some problems were more appropriately handled by a small group of persons already well acquainted with the subject, pooling their experience and obtaining any information they needed in varied, but less formal ways. Occasionally a working party was provided with a 'Steering Committee', often of important officers, which the working party might consult on various aspects of its problem as occasion required.

It is not surprising, then, that departments should see the advantages of this form of inquiry, especially for investigating matters demanding personal knowledge, and they quickly began to make free use of it for

26 1931 Non-Parl., Bd. of Education.
27 1938 Non-Parl., Bd. of Education.
28 1959 Non-Parl., Min. of Education.
29 1963 Non-Parl., Min. of Education.

normal 'civil' questions. Thus the problems to be faced and the re-organization required by certain industries after the war were eminently suitable for investigation in this way. After the First World War this work was done by departmental committees, which reported on the position of the Textile Trades, Iron and Steel Trades, Electrical and Engineering Trades and the Shipbuilding and Housing Industries. But from 1946, when the first report by a working party was published, to 1948, sixteen such inquiries were carried out by working parties appointed by the Board of Trade.

The obvious advantages these less formal methods of inquiry offered as to size, membership, scope and methods of work led to their adoption, sometimes under other names, by other departments. Between 1955 and 1964 the Ministry of Education set up twenty-one. Those appointed by the Ministry of Health included working parties on *Health Visiting,* 1956, and on *Social Workers in the Local Authority Health and Welfare Services,* 1959, and the Home Office set one up on *Legal Aid in Criminal Proceedings,* 1962–63, while the Working Group on the *Proposal for a Fixed Channel Link,* 1963, and the Technical Advisory Panel on *Research in the Iron and Steel Industry,* 1963, show the uses to which they could be put. The variety of subject matter and method affected the nature and structure of the reports; the working papers, including contributions to the discussions made orally by persons asked to give them, are not usually published, but the reports often contain memoranda and other papers which should not be overlooked.

Annual Reports and Statistical Series. The annual reports of various departments and bodies created by Parliament are the chief, indeed the indispensable sources of information on the particular fields they cover, not least because they form a running series over a period of years. Some of them, as we have seen, are required by statute to be laid before Parliament. Others are presented to it 'By Command': for example, those of the Commissioners of Customs and the Commissioners of Inland Revenue, of the Department of Health and Social Security and the British Broadcasting Corporation. Others are not brought to the House, but published by departmental authority. These include the reports of the Council of Industrial Design and of the Covent Garden Market Authority. Some of these series have been in existence for many years, sometimes unchanged in name, sometimes with such alteration of name as was required by the change in the title of the ministry or department responsible.

That of the Commissioners of Inland Revenue has been issued for over a century, of the Commissioners of Customs for over a century, those of the Inspector of Factories, the Department of Health and Social Security (formerly Ministry of Health and other predecessors) for over a century. Some of them are statistical, like those of the Registrar

General, the Statistical Abstract and the Annual Statement of Trade, whose great merit is that they provide continuous records for over a century. (A list of the most important of these series in the nineteenth century and their appropriate paper numbers is given in appendix 4 of the *Select List of British Parliamentary Papers, 1833–1899*. Lists for the twentieth century can be found in *A Breviate of Parliamentary Papers, 1900–1916*, the Breviate covering the years 1940–54 and the *Select List, 1955–1964*).

It should not, however, be assumed that the value of annual reports is limited to their statistics, or to the record of the work of administration; on the contrary, they may contain supplementary reports or accounts of special investigations of importance not only in a particular scientific and technical field, but also in public policy. Of this, two examples widely separated in time will suffice. The first consists of two memoranda, vital in the public health campaign, by Dr Southwood Smith in 1837–38 and 1839 on *Physical Causes of Sickness and Mortality to which the Poor are Particularly Exposed* and *Fever in Metropolitan Unions*, in the appendices to the fourth and fifth annual reports of the Poor Law Commission; the second is the great paper on the organization of a national health service by Dr Arthur Newsholme in his annual report as Chief Medical Officer to the Local Government Board, issued as a supplement to that department's annual report.[30]

Other Official Papers. Besides the reports of these committees of inquiry and the annual reports, there are a large number of other departmental or official publications, some of them forming a considerable series. They include: (1) The published awards of the Industrial Court, the Civil Service Arbitration Tribunal and the Industrial Disputes Tribunal on wages disputes, as well as the larger reports of the Courts of Inquiry into major industrial disputes. They also include selected decisions of the commissioner (formerly the Umpire) on appeal cases brought before him on insurance claims and disallowances. (2) Similar to these, in a different field, are selected decisions on income tax cases. (3) Large numbers of Statutory Instruments (or Statutory Rules and Orders, as they were formerly called). These arise from the delegated powers of legislation, i.e. the authority to make orders having the effect of law on particular matters, which Parliament has granted to various Departments. Papers in group (1) and some in group (3) arise from state activities which did not exist in the nineteenth century.

Another important group consists of *research papers*. Departments have become more active and have exercised more initiative in research matters within their field of responsibility. There is an increasing flow of studies from their research organizations and units, some of which

30   1918 Cd.9169, xi.

are long-standing, others comparatively new. These vary from man-power studies by the Department of Employment and Productivity, studies on population by the General Register Offfce, on public health and medical subjects by the Department of Health and Social Security, on delinquency and persistent offenders by the Home Office. A list show-ing the range of some of the reports will be found in the *Select List, 1955–1964,* App. II.

Finally, there is a steady stream of *information papers* proceeding from government departments and other bodies. They include reports on special studies arranged by the Medical Research Council, technical reports on building questions and scientific and practical advice by the Ministry of Agriculture. The publicity departments of the separate ministries issue a wide range of informative pamphlets and individual reports of factual, scientific and general value, such as *Living in Flats,* 1952 Non-Parl. (Ministry of Housing and Local Government); *Feeding the One to Fives,* 1950 Non-Parl. (Ministry of Health); *Poultry Breeding,* 1960 (Ministry of Agriculture and Fisheries). These are designed to bring first-class information from the departments to the factory, farm and home, but important and essential though this growing volume of literature is, and though it may arise from bodies Parliament has set up, or instructions it has given, it is obviously different in character from those printed papers necessary for the work of Parliament itself.

(c)   *Command and Non-Parliamentary Papers*

We have seen that some of these classes of departmental and official papers are formally presented to Parliament as Command papers and that some are not. This distinction of form has a profound effect on their arrangement. Before 1921 parliamentary papers included nearly all documents of importance; few of those significant for policy were issued as non-parliamentary papers. The official description of non-parliamen-tary papers was then simply 'Official Publications'. Since 1921 there has been a fundamental change in the situation. The immediate cause of this was the difficulties which arose from the Free List. The House and Com-mand papers, known together as the sessional papers, were distributed free to Members and to a number of bodies and organizations both at home and abroad, and the expense of this practice had engaged the attention of many committees on economy campaigns of the govern-ment after the First World War, when the Treasury issued the important Circular No. 38/21. This instructed departments to modify their practice of issuing departmental papers as parliamentary ones, and directed that henceforth papers were not to be presented by Command unless the matter dealt with was likely to be the subject of early legislation or the papers were otherwise essential to Members of Parliament as a whole to enable them to discharge their responsibilities.

The initial decision in each individual case was left to the departments, and the result was greatly to reduce the numbers of departmental papers presented and therefore going on to the free list. The immediate effect was to transfer a number of papers such as Colonial reports, certain annual reports of departments and ad hoc bodies—the Board of Control, the Development Commission and the Mint—statistical returns, census reports and the Annual Statement of Trade, as given in the list submitted by the Controller of the Stationery Office to the Select Committee on *Publications and Debates,* 1923.[31] But the long-run effects were more far-reaching and went beyond what seems to have been originally contemplated, for not only were regular and routine reports of the kind included in the Controller's list affected, but also policy documents of importance. For the Treasury rule had to be interpreted and applied to the greatly increasing flow of reports from these outside investigating bodies—the departmental, advisory and consultative committees, etc. The result has been greatly to reduce the proportion of departmental and similar papers presented and to increase the number and proportion not presented and therefore not in the sessional sets or indexes. The non-parliamentary group thus includes reports on public policy made after careful and elaborate inquiry which before 1921 would have been treated as parliamentary. The old term 'official' was an inadequate description and the negative term 'non-parliamentary' came into use to describe them.

The combined effect, then, of the development of the work of departmental investigating bodies and the Treasury rule has been to introduce confusion into the arrangement of parliamentary papers. It would not always be possible for departments to foresee at the time of publication whether a paper would become the 'subject of *early* legislation'. The first report of the Onslow Commission on Voluntary Hospitals (1925) was published as a Command paper, but in 1926 the commission was informed that financial circumstances would make it impracticable to find the money required for the proposals. The commission's final report in 1928 was published as a non-parliamentary paper and is therefore separated from its fellow. Sometimes the community, through Parliament, the departments and the various committees, is really working at a vexed problem over a number of years, yet some of the reports on the subject are Commands, others are non-parliamentary, so that the series cannot be found as a whole in the sessional papers or sessional indexes. Reports from the Advisory Housing Panel and the Advisory Council on Housing in 1918 and 1919 were presented; but a report in 1932 of the Consultative Council on *Steps necessary to Secure that State Aided Houses will in future be let only to Persons of the Working Classes* and two reports by the Central Housing Committee in 1936 and 1937 on *Rural Housing* were not presented. Thus of the papers on

31   1923 (140) viii.

Water Supply issued between 1917 and 1919 six are Command papers, three are House papers and six are non-parliamentary papers. While the Willink Report, 1957, on the future numbers of medical practitioners is non-parliamentary, both the McNair Report on the recruitment to the dental profession and the Pilkington Report on doctors' and dentists' remuneration are Commands and are in the sessional series. And for reasons given below, some important reports on the coal industry have been published by the Coal Board itself and are neither in the sessional nor the non-parliamentary papers, but outside both.

A further complication arises from the treatment of minutes of evidence. As we have seen, select committees and Royal Commissions print their evidence, i.e. the formal hearings, but the Treasury rule has been applied so that the report of a commission may be presented as a Command while the evidence on which the report is apparently based is non-parliamentary. In such cases the report is to be found in the sessional papers and indexes, but the evidence is not. In addition, departmental committees, or the departments which appoint them, have exercised their freedom not to publish their evidence, so there may be no printed version available. But the evidence on which a report is based may be at least as valuable as the report itself, and it may be important to know what evidence was not taken or considered at all. While there are minor inquiries in which this is not of great moment, there are others in which the historian would have preferred to assess the evidence for himself.[32]

The completeness of the sessional bound sets—Parliament's own papers, if one may use the term—once regarded as containing all the papers on public policy, has thus been weakened. At the outset the Treasury criteria—the likelihood of early legislation and the need for papers by the members as a whole—must have seemed administratively sensible and practical. In the operation, they have sometimes put the scholars at a disadvantage.

32 The evidence issued as non-parliamentary papers is sometimes published in folio, sometimes in octavo. This makes some difficulties for librarians in arranging and shelving and for researchers using an open access system. In the inter-war years, while presented reports, whether of commissions or committees, were in octavo, the evidence was commonly in folio, as in the case of the Macmillan Committee on *Finance and Industry,* 1931, the Holman Gregory Commission on *Unemployment Insurance,* 1932, and the Barlow Commission on the *Distribution of the Industrial Population,* 1940. The evidence, papers, etc., of the Simon Commission on *Population,* 1940, and of the Fulton Commission on the *Civil Service,* 1968, is non-parliamentary; some of those of the former are octavo, some folio, while those of the latter are octavo. The evidence on the *Civil Service* to the Tomlin Commission, 1931, and to the Priestley Commission, 1955, was issued as non-parliamentary, the former in folio, the latter in octavo. The evidence of the Radcliffe Committee on the *Monetary System,* 1959, is non-parliamentary and in folio; that of the Robbins Committee on *Higher Education,* 1962–63, was presented by command and issued in octavo.

(d) *Papers of Nationalized Industries and Government Institutions*

Further developments have led to the publication of papers which are neither parliamentary nor, in the sense defined above, non-parliamentary. Just as the growth of new forms of departmental activity gave rise to departmental and advisory committees, so the extension of state functions has led to the establishment of state institutions and undertakings which make inquiries, issue and publish reports and papers independently of H.M.S.O. Some of these institutions are not new, e.g. the museums and the Ordnance Survey, and material thus issued varies from maps, museum guides and reproductions to technical publications. But the matter was brought to a head by the establishment of nationalized industries which have independent trading functions and do not necessarily come within the scope of H.M.S.O. for their publishing needs, save in respect of annual reports they may be required to present to Parliament. Papers concerning the high policies and plans of great industries, such as the Coal Board's *Plan for Coal* and *Investing in Coal,* the Transport Commission's reports on *Electrification of Railways* and on *Canals and Inland Waterways* or the Gas Council's *Fuel for the Nation,* have been published by the industries themselves.

Some of these policy documents, such as those named, are neither printed, published nor sold by H.M.S.O. and do not appear in the Consolidated Lists or Catalogues of Government Publications. A small number, such as the Fleck Report on *Organisation,* are published independently but sold through H.M.S.O. and are entered in its lists with a note to that effect. But this practice of industries, nationalized because they were thought to be vital to the British economy, may result in taking some of their important papers out of the series of the nation's papers, either parliamentary or non-parliamentary, and therefore out of the indexes and lists. For the most part their publications will have to be sought in the British National Bibliography. It ought not to be impossible to arrange that papers of this class should find their way into the main body of papers, if not by presentation, then by being published or at least sold by H.M.S.O.

(e) *House of Lords Papers*

In this Guide attention is directed in the *first instance* to the papers of the House of Commons, for good reasons of convenience. Generally speaking, House of Lords papers take the same form as those of the Commons—procedure papers, the Journals, the Debates, House papers and Command papers. Its sessional papers were bound and indexed in the nineteenth century on somewhat the same lines as those of the Commons, but fewer sets have been preserved. Fortunately, however, each House 'communicated' documents to the other House, so that a large number of Lords papers are in the Commons volumes and have Commons numbers. Thus it is only for Lords papers not communicated and therefore not in the Commons set that the Lords volumes need be consulted. On the other hand, many of the nineteenth-century volumes contain Command papers also in the Commons set, but since 1900 these have been omitted and the number of volumes has therefore dwindled. The only duplication now remaining consists of the reports of joint committees of both Houses which, as they are appointed by both, naturally report to each House. And, while some important investigations on matters of public policy have been made by Lords select committees, such as that on the *Resumption of Cash Payments,* 1819, those on the condition of work of chimney sweeps in the first half and on *Sweating* in the second half of the century (though the reports of the latter were communicated), in the main their work has been concerned with evidence and reports on bills.

The House of Lords Record Office. The Record Office possesses a large collection of original papers presented to the House of Lords. It was customary, probably from the seventeenth century, to preserve them in a simple continuous series arranged chronologically. The papers for the period 1497 to 1690 are bound in 340 red files; those from 1690 to date are mainly preserved in 8,000 box files and arranged in order of presentation. The printed series of Lords papers is merely a continuation of these original papers. For the period after 1800, the printed series of parliamentary papers for both Lords and Commons can be usefully supplemented by the unprinted papers preserved in the Victoria Tower. See M. F. Bond, *Guide to the Records of Parliament,* H.M.S.O., 1971.

PART II

How to Find Them

Groups of parliamentary papers are bound together to form separate series of volumes. These series differ from one another in size and arrangement according to the nature of the contents and to the historical processes through which they came to be preserved.

I. Papers Relating to the Agenda, Proceedings and Debates of the House

(a) *Agenda, Votes and Proceedings*

The papers on the procedure of the House are issued separately. In the British Museum they are bound up as follows: (1) votes and proceedings; (2) divisions; (3) notices of motions; questions and orders of the day; (4) private business.

(b) *The Journals and the Indexes*

The Journals are printed at the end of each session, together with a sessional index. Up to 1835 (vol. 90) they are in double folio; after that date, except for occasional ones, they are in folio. The earlier volumes contain more than one session, but from 1833 (vol. 88) they usually contain the record of one session; if there are two sessions within one year, the second session is included in the same volume. They are numbered in an unbroken series throughout. Since 1880 the sessional index has also been consolidated into separately issued decennial ones.

The General Indexes for the Journals of the eighteenth century were compiled by five men: Cunningham, Flexman, Forster, Moore and Dunn, four of whom worked individually on a particular period, producing four different types of alphabetical indexes. The fifth, Dunn, followed Moore's index, with certain exceptions. The periods covered by these indexes are:

1547–1659	vols. 1–7	Cunningham's index
1660–97	vols. 8–11	Flexman's index
1697–1714	vols. 12–17	Forster's index
1714–74	vols. 18–34	Moore's index
1774–1800	vols. 35–55	Dunn's index

In 1818 John Rickman began supervising the production of the indexes, using Moore's index as the basis for his plans, and all succeeding indexes were uniform in construction. Two volumes of revised indexes were published to bring the earlier ones into line with the nineteenth-century ones. Those of Cunningham, Flexman and Forster were revised in one volume covering the period 1547 to 1714 and the two indexes by Dunn in one volume from 1774 to 1800. Before the regular decennial indexes beginning in 1880 there were five general indexes for the nineteenth century: 1801–20, 1820–37, 1837–52, 1852–65 and 1866–79.

There is thus a set of uniform indexes to the Journals. Where, however, libraries possess only the first group of indexes, named above, for the Journals before the nineteenth century, the reader must be aware of the differences in compilation so that he is not confused in moving from one to the other.

(c) *Parliamentary History and the Debates*

There are thirty-six octavo volumes of the *Parliamentary History, 1066–1803,* and five series of Debates covering different periods. Each volume is numbered in the series to which it belongs.

			Title page and dates of change of title or series
1803–20	41 vols.	1st Series	Cobbett's Parliamentary Debates. Parliamentary Debates (1812, vol. 23).
1820–30	25 vols.	2nd Series	Parliamentary Debates (Accession of George IV). Hansard's Parliamentary Debates (1829, vol. 21).
1830–91	350 vols.	3rd Series	Hansard's Parliamentary Debates (Accession of William IV).
1892–1908	77 vols.	4th Series	Parliamentary Debates (Authorized).
1909–		5th Series	Parliamentary Debates (Official). Parliamentary Debates (Hansard) (1943).

The debates are now published daily and weekly, and when a volume is complete they are bound in sessional volumes. Each volume has an index of its own, but the last volume of the session contains a complete sessional index.

In 1919 there began an annual supplementary series of volumes containing the official reports of debates in standing committees.

II. House of Commons Papers and Command Papers (Sessional Papers)

(a) *Collections, Indexes and List*

Before the nineteenth century there was no systematic way of preserving the papers, so that the records and the collections which have come down to us cannot be regarded as complete. Many papers must have passed out of the custody of the House before efforts were made to preserve them. Those stored in the House were burnt in the fire of 1834.

There is however, an extensive collection in manuscript form in the House of Lords Record Office (see p. 19). Some papers were printed and published by order of the House of Commons (see 4 below).[1] Many of these papers are in the House of Lords Record Office, in the British Museum and in the following bound collections.

(i) *Reports and other Papers in the Journals.* Papers laid on the table are entered in the Journals. Before the nineteenth century many reports were printed in full in the body of the Journals, and references to them can be traced in the indexes under such headings as 'accounts and papers', 'reports', 'committees', 'House' and 'printing'. By 1800 the Journals had become so bulky that a selection of reports made by the Speaker was transferred to an appendix. This ended in 1835 because of the duplication with the bound sessional sets.

(ii) *First Series, 1715–1801.* This series comprises a reprint of a selection of the reports which had been printed in the Journals or had been printed separately. There are fifteen volumes, together with an index. The index contains a list of the reports of committees which were inserted in the Journals but not considered of sufficient importance to be included among the reprints.[2]

(iii) *Abbot Collection, 1731–1800.* The collection comprises 111 folio volumes of separately printed papers which were in store at the time of the reprint which formed the First Series. It is by no means complete, but as the papers have been preserved in this way, they are easy to handle and read. Charles Abbot ordered that they should be gathered together and bound. The material was arranged in three groups—bills, reports, accounts and papers—each in chronological order with a serial numbering. There is an index to this collection entitled *Catalogue of Papers Printed by Order of the House of Commons, 1731–1800* (1807; reprinted

---

1 Official sales continued until well past the middle of the eighteenth century, and although the precise period when it ceased is not known, the last paper with the publisher's imprint was in 1771. However, sales continued unofficially. Between 1750 and 1835 all reports and printed papers of the House (except the votes, the public sale of which was authorized) reached the public through members to their friends or through the Speaker, 'or else by traffic connived at rather than expressly sanctioned, in which the officers, messengers and doorkeepers of the House who received copies of these Papers as their perquisites, retailed them to the public through the medium of the person whose business it was to sell and distribute the Votes'. *Publication of Printed Papers,* Sel. Cttee., App. 3; 1837 (286) xiii; and *Publications and Debates,* Sel. Cttee., Librarian's memo, p. 77; 1914–16 (321) iv.

Unofficial copies of reports, especially of best sellers such as the Bullion Report, had always been sold. They ceased in 1890 when by letters patent direct assignment was made of the copyright of all government publications to the Controller of the Stationery Office. Third Ann. Rep., p. 18; 1890 C.5995, xxvi.

2 For more details of the First Series, see Appendix I.

H.M.S.O. 1954). There is a set in the House of Commons, one in the House of Lords Library, one in the British Museum and an incomplete one at University College, London. There is also a microprint edition of the collection.[3]

(iv) *Sessional List, 1701–50.* Sheila Lambert, *List of House of Commons Sessional Papers, 1701–1750* (1968) is an invaluable list of eighteenth century papers arranged in sessional order. The preface gives details of the kinds of papers, their printing and publication. For each session there is information as to where these papers can be found—the Journals, the Votes, the British Museum, the First Series, etc.

(b) *Bound Sessional Sets, 1801–continuing*

Since 1801, at the end of each session the papers which have been before Parliament are bound into volumes to form a series which has become known as the bound sets of sessional papers.[4] Each session's papers are arranged in four groups—bills, reports of committees, reports of commissioners and accounts and papers—the papers within each group being bound in alphabetical subject order. These papers now bear one of three series of numbers.

(i) *Bills.* Bills were first numbered with the House papers. In the sessional index for 1854 they were listed separately with their own sessional numbers and appear as the first numerical group in all succeeding sessional indexes.

(ii) *House of Commons Papers.* A fresh series of paper numbers is started each session. From the commencement of the bound set in 1801, a 'printer's number'[5] was placed in the 'bottom-corner' of all House papers, and when the first alphabetical index was printed for the session 1814–15 this number was inserted in round brackets (possibly to distinguish it from the pagination of the bound volumes) and was used as the sessional index reference number to the paper in the bound sets. For example, 1814–15 (119) vii, 117 indicates the session, the paper number of the session, the bound volume number and the page within the bound volume.

(iii) *Command Papers.* Historically, 'By Command' signified that the Crown had exercised its right to command its commissioners to present a document to Parliament or that it had commanded it to be presented

---

3 For more details of the Abbot Collection, see Appendix I.
4 K. A. C. Parsons, *A Checklist of the British Parliamentary Papers (Bound Set), 1801–1950* (Cambridge 1958), shows the number of volumes in each session and the numbers of Command papers which were either not printed or appeared in the Lords sets only.
5 See Hansard's 'Explanation', *General Index, 1801–1832*, p. 1.

in response to a petition from Parliament for information. Papers now presented 'By Command' bear both a legend to that effect and a serial command number and are listed in the sessional indexes as command papers.[6] But while a fresh series of House paper numbers is started each session, command numbers extend over many sessions. Owing to historical circumstances, for a period in the nineteenth century this simple plan was not followed. By the end of the eighteenth century the printing of the papers was well organized by the Printer to the House, Luke Hansard, 1799–1828, whose appointment was the prerogative of the Speaker. The Speaker also had some responsibility in deciding what was printed, appending his signature to the manuscript and stating the number of copies to be printed. Between the years 1801–35 most papers, with the exception of many from the Foreign Office, but including those of Royal Commissions of inquiry, have a printer's number, indicating that they were printed by Hansard. A change took place in 1833, when the Treasury and the Home Office by-passed the Hansard monopoly through the Stationery Office, and papers were printed by a firm it named. That further inroads were not made quickly at this time was due to the operation of what L. G. Hansard called 'the parliamentary rule that no *printed paper* should be received by the House'.[7] But this difficulty was resolved by a recommendation in the report of the House of Lords Select Committee on *Office of the Clerk of the Parliaments* (1834 (HL.55) xxi) which was accepted as a resolution in the House of Commons and was entered in the Journal (vol. 90, 30 Aug. 1835) as follows:

> All Parliamentary Papers presented by Command of His Majesty in a printed form be received, kept and distributed with those presented in manuscript form pursuant to Act of Parliament or by Order of the House.

---

6   The Foreign Office had its own printing press, from which papers were printed before being brought to the House. In the early nineteenth century, papers concerning conventions and treaties continued to be delivered 'at the door of the House' and they were included in the bound sessional sets without paper numbers. For an explanation of these peculiarities see G. E. and H. G. Harrison, *The House of Harrison* (1914); J. Rickman's evidence before the Select Committee on Printing Done for the House, p. 51; 1828 (520) iv; Temperley and Penson, *A Century of Diplomatic Blue Books;* Sheila Lambert, 'Presentation of Parliamentary Papers by the Foreign Office', *Institute of Historical Research Bulletin,* XXIII (1950), 76–83.
7   P. and G. Ford, *Luke Graves Hansard's Diary, 1814–1841* (Oxford 1962), p. 152. Hansard comments that 'These documents [Command papers] were, from the earliest period of their forming part of the means of legislative information, laid before both Houses of Parliament in MS, and were generally ordered by each House to be printed for their respective use. This practice may be traced as far back as the reign of Queen Anne.' Ibid., p. 151.

Confusion was increased as more papers were thus presented and were without a printer's number. To rectify this the Select Committee on *Printed Papers* (1835 (392) xviii) recommended that a committee should be set up to assist the Speaker as to the delivery and proper classification of the papers. Those which bore the legend 'Ordered by the House of Commons to be Printed' had already been given House paper numbers, but the papers presented in a printed form had been left unnumbered. These sixty-seven were assigned command numbers [1] to [67]—the square brackets possibly being used to distinguish them from the round brackets of the House paper numbers.[8] Since the papers had already been issued the numbers were not on them, and unfortunately the practice of not printing the command number on them was continued until 1869, so that up to that date it is not possible to identify a command paper simply from the command number given in the index.

An interesting example of how this works is shown by the numbering of the reports of the Royal Commission on the Poor Laws. They were ordered to be printed in 1834 and have the House number (44). The First Report and Appendices A and B of the Royal Commission on the Irish Poor Laws were ordered to be printed and have the House paper number (369), while the rest of the papers had the legend 'Presented by Command' and were given command numbers in 1836. And for the same reasons the papers of the Royal Commission on Municipal Corporations, England and Wales, 1835–37, have the House paper number (116) while the Irish and Scottish Royal Commissions have command numbers.

As the command papers had been first numbered serially through three sessions, this numbering was continued through the succeeding sessional lists until 1869. In 1870 the number was printed on the paper; a code—C for Command—was added to the square bracket, and a new series begun. There are now five series:

1833–68/69	[1] to [4222]	Not printed on the papers.
1870–99	[C.1] to [C.9550]	Number printed on the paper and C added as an extra code.
1900–18	[Cd.1] to [Cd.9239]	Marks the beginning of the century to the end of the First World War. Code changed to Cd.
1919–55/56	[Cmd.1] to Cmd.9889	Marks the beginning of the inter-war period. Code changed to Cmd.
1956/57	Cmnd.1 continuing	Code changed to Cmnd.

8   See Explanation in *General Index, 1832–44,* 'where papers are presented to the House in a printed form, thus [149]', and the *General Index, 1852–53 to 1868–69,* 'Papers Presented by Command are distinguished thus [3212].'

The form of reference in the indexes to the command papers is, for example, 1900 [Cd.40] v, 240. In 1922 the square brackets ceased to be printed on the paper, and in 1950–51 they were omitted from the sessional index. They really became redundant in 1870 when the use of the letter code began.[9]

(c) *Other Collections: Petitions, State Papers*

The bound sessional sets can be usefully supplemented by three other collections.

(i) *Papers Preserved in the House of Lords Record Office.* See page 19.

(ii) *Petitions.* Before 1833 petitions had been printed as an appendix to the Votes, but as the numbers increased—there were over 24,000 in the five years ending 1831—this became very bulky. Between 1833 and 1910 the reports from the Select Committee on *Petitions* are bound in a separate series. (See bound volumes in the British Museum.)

(iii) *State Papers.* This collection 'comprises the principal documents which have been made public relating to the political and commercial affairs of the nations and their relations with each other from the termination of the war 1814' (advertisement in the volumes). Though originally a private venture edited by Lewis Hertslet, the librarian at the Foreign Office, it eventually became official. Since 1968 State papers have been listed in the annual catalogue under the name of the Foreign and Commonwealth Office.

(d) *Indexes to Bound Sets of Sessional Papers*

(i) *Sessional Index to Commons Papers.* This index is the last volume of the sessional bound set and is the chief means of access to the bound volumes of the session until it is consolidated into a decennial index.[10] Except for such changes as developed with the passage of time, these indexes contain: List of the Bound Volumes, Numerical List of Bills, Numerical List of Papers, Numerical List of Command Papers, Alphabetical Subject Index, Chairman Index since 1959–60.

(ii) *General Alphabetical Indexes.* Except for the interruption in the war years of 1914–18 and 1939–45 there have been decennial indexes since 1870. Before that date indexes were published at irregular inter-

---

9   The necessity for a periodic change in the code might be overcome by enclosing a *sessional* Command number in square brackets.

10   Access is made more difficult when there is a long time lag between publication and binding, and between binding and indexing. A suggestion has been made that parliamentary papers should be arranged numerically in three groups—bills, House of Commons papers and command papers—and bound as each volume is completed, thus giving immediate access through H.M.S.O. catalogue.

vals,[11] but they were consolidated into three volumes covering 1801–52 and one volume for the period 1852–53 to 1868–69. There is a general alphabetical index for 1852–99, but its usefulness is limited, since by an error on the part of the compilers, the references to the paper numbers were not included. The five general indexes published up to 1850 are clear guides for the limited periods they cover. The one for 1845–50 (698) is very bulky because Hansard carried out the wishes of the committee by indexing reports buried in the appendices of some papers (see p. 54) giving them a reference number, e.g. (in 192). For the half-century the most useful indexes are the three consolidated volumes for 1801–52.

A little difficulty is sometimes experienced in the use of these consolidated volumes when a search is being made for reports. This is because volume two, entitled *Reports,* deals with the reports of committees, but reports of commissioners are listed separately with the accounts and papers in volume three, so that if one is not sure whether the report required is from a committee or a commission, both volumes must be consulted.[12] In all the other alphabetical indexes, the entries under the subject headings are arranged in the four groups corresponding to the arrangement of the papers in the bound volumes: (1) bills; (2) reports of committees; (3) reports of commissioners; (4) accounts and papers. While this method of arranging the entries has obvious advantages, nevertheless a little care is necessary to ensure that the searcher is looking in the right group. Papers for Scotland and Ireland are listed separately under each heading.

For the twentieth century, the five decennials for 1900–49 have been consolidated into one volume by the librarian of the House of Commons and printed by H. M. Stationery Office. This index includes a table showing the numbers of papers issued during this period, a long explanatory preface on the papers and an appendix giving a list of short titles of bills.

Indexes compiled at different dates for more than a century and a half naturally show some differences in the way they are made up and these may sometimes trouble the user, but the general plan is much the same throughout. In structure they are really a mixture of an alphabetical and a subject index, but this arises partly from the nature of the documents, for parliamentary papers normally have no 'author' and many of them no 'title' in the ordinary sense of these words, the 'titles' themselves may be misleading.[13] Thus papers on educational subjects are entered under 'Education'; but papers on election petitions appear under

11 See Appendix I, p. 57.
12 The Select Lists and the three volumes of Breviates of parliamentary papers covering the period 1833–1964 bring together the reports on the various subjects, whether those of committees or commissions (see p. 78).
13 For further details, see Introduction, *Select List, 1833–99,* pp. ix–xi.

'Elections' in one index and under the respective boroughs in another. These variations reveal the style of the compilers of the different dates and show the contemporary emphasis on a particular group of papers on a particular subject, but they provide no fundamental obstacle to the use of the indexes.

(iii) *Catalogue of Government Publications*. Formerly called the *Consolidated List,* this is the annual sales list of H. M. Stationery Office; the first part deals with parliamentary and the second with non-parliamentary papers.[14] Daily lists and monthly catalogues are issued and at the end of the year are consolidated into the annual catalogue. In it the parliamentary papers are arranged as in the numerical part of the sessional indexes, and it therefore provides access to them until they are bound and the sessional index is in print. It should be noted that whereas the sessional indexes relate to the parliamentary sessional dates, the catalogue refers to the *calendar year*.

III. Non-Parliamentary Papers

The annual catalogue is the only index for the non-parliamentary papers. In it the papers are arranged under the department of origin, and the departments are arranged in alphabetical order. There is a separate section listing Royal Commissions, which includes the information regarding their minutes of evidence and other papers which have not been presented to Parliament as command papers. Each catalogue contains an alphabetical index of chairmen, authors and the titles of the papers. These indexes are now cumulated every five years. This is the general layout of the *lists* from 1921–53 and the *catalogue* from 1954 onwards. Parliamentary papers were put on sale from 1836,[15] and sales lists go back to that date.[16]

From 1968 the references to non-parliamentary papers, etc., are to the standard book number (SBN); previously an H.M.S.O. code number was used. There are no official bound sets of non-parliamentary

14 Since 1949 the non-parliamentary section has been enlarged to include duplicate entries of parliamentary papers other than acts and bills. This has the advantage of indicating the departmental origin of Command papers.
15 *Publication and Sale of Printed Papers,* Sel. Cttee. Rep.; 1835 (61)(392) xviii.
16 The British Museum's copy, printed in 1854, gives the papers back to that date. In 1882 the present arrangement of the list began to emerge in two lists entitled *Official Publications* and *Parliamentary Papers,* and by 1894, when they took the form of quarterly lists, the general arrangement of the non-parliamentary papers under the departments of origin was established. From 1922 to 1953 it was called the *Consolidated List*. The title 'non-parliamentary' appears in the *Consolidated List* in 1924. From 1922–34 minutes of evidence of Royal Commissions will be found either under department of origin, or under the heading 'Royal Commission' in the 'Miscellaneous' group.

papers, and in view of their range, variety and volume, this is hardly surprising. This was less serious when they consisted of and were correctly described as 'official' papers than it is when an increasing number of important 'policy' papers are included among them. For this reason, and because it is not practicable for most libraries to order them 'complete', as they can sessional papers, but only individually or in groups, collections of non-parliamentary papers are often deficient and not well arranged. The British Museum as a 'copyright' library does aim at 'completion' and keeps them in groups under department of origin, and in date order within each department. Southampton University shelves its non-parliamentary papers first by calendar year and then by department of origin to correspond with the arrangement in the annual catalogue.

It is necessary to stress once again that much trouble can be saved by being fully aware of the consequences of the Treasury circular of 1921. They are, of course, threefold. First, certain classes of papers which were parliamentary before that date and were entered in the sessional indexes are non-parliamentary afterwards and must be sought for in the consolidated list or annual catalogue. Secondly, as we have seen, the papers on a particular topic—all of them 'policy' documents—may sometimes be parliamentary, and sometimes non-parliamentary. Further—and perhaps this is the most confusing of all—the report of a Royal Commission will, of course, be parliamentary and recorded in the sessional indexes, but the evidence may be non-parliamentary and not so recorded: for this the annual catalogue must be consulted. In addition, while before 1921 it was common practice for the various days of evidence to be collected and presented in a volume or volumes, since 1921 evidence is often printed and issued in separate 'days' and not later collected into volumes. Since such inquiries may spread over two or more calendar years, it may therefore be important to check that one has the complete set of evidence before one.[17]

The Royal Commission on *Local Government in England* increased the difficulties by issuing its written evidence (1967–69) in twenty-one separate parts unnumbered in any way and without any symbol to indicate their sequence. The H.M.S.O. annual catalogue simply lists them as published.

IV. House of Lords Papers

The Lords indexes, though their detailed history is different, follow much the same pattern as those of the Commons, except that from

17   The Breviates and the *Select List, 1955–1964* are designed to meet the difficulty by bringing together all the reports, evidence and other papers of a particular investigation, whether they are parliamentary or non-parliamentary.

1900–20 they contain a fictitious element in that they include references to command papers presented to the Lords but not actually bound in their sets. They provide a useful check with the Commons indexes, particularly in identifying those communicated documents which underwent a slight change of title during their passage from one House to another. Occasionally there is an untidiness which can be picked up in the Lords set. The notorious example of this is Chadwick's famous report on the *Sanitary Condition of the Labouring Population,* 1842. Although the title page states that it was presented to both Houses by command, it is not in the Commons set or indexes, but it is in the Lords set and index, though without either a command or a House number. The supplementary report on *Interment in Towns* is included in the Commons papers, and in error its number is often given as the number of the *General Report.* Mr Parsons' checklist (see p. 79) names thirty-five command papers absent from the Commons set but found in the Lords papers.

The general alphabetical indexes to the Lords papers are as follows:

1801–1837	*General Index*
1801–1859	*General Index* (reprinted H.M.S.O., 1938)
1859–1870	*General Index*
1871–1884/85	*General Index*
1886–1920	*Sessional Indexes*
1921–	*Sessional Lists*

The H.M.S.O. catalogues enter Lords papers in a numerical list and in the alphabetical index, thus providing access to them until the sessional list is printed in the form of contents pages for the bound volumes. They provide the only alphabetical index to the Lords papers.

V.   Location of Bound Sessional Sets

The most complete sets of House of Lords papers are in the House itself, the British Museum and in some government departments. The most complete sets of Commons papers are in the Houses of Parliament, in some government departments, and in the British Museum, Bodleian, Cambridge, Edinburgh, Trinity College, Dublin,[18] London School of Economics libraries and the Ford Collection at Southampton University. Other libraries with collections of varying degrees of completeness include some universities and several municipal libraries.

VI.   Collections of Reprinted Papers in Subject Order

Early in the nineteenth century Hansard made up five sets of printed papers arranged in subject order, amounting to 362 volumes in each

18   For the recommendation that these should be deposit libraries for parliamentary papers, see *State of Printed Reports and Papers,* p. 4; 1825 (516) v.

set (see p. 50). The Irish University Press is publishing two collections of reprints of nineteenth century papers in approximately 1,200 volumes. The first of these collections consists of 1,000 volumes (publication completed 1971) which include the most important reports selected from those given in Hansard's catalogue and for the relevant fields from the *Select List, 1833–1899,* arranged in subject order: agriculture, government, health, industrial revolution, education, social problems, anthropology, poor law, etc. This collection also includes all the reports and papers on slavery and on Australia, Canada and New Zealand, as well as selected reports and papers from colonies in Africa, the East Indies and the West Indies. The second of the IUP collections (the *Area Studies Series*—publication commenced 1971) consists of 200 volumes devoted to various countries: United States of America, China and Japan, Russia, and Central and South America. This collection contains *all* the material pertaining to a particular country except bills, estimates, and small statistical returns (in which that country appears with other nations).

PART III

How to Use Them

It is no doubt true that the best teacher in the handling and use of parliamentary papers is experience, but anyone confronted with the work of one of the great commissions and its volumes of evidence may well wish to be sure that he has picked up all he can of the methods which others have found useful. We shall therefore set out, with the aid of illustrations, the ways in which the papers should be approached, the questions which must be asked and the points which must be looked at if work on them is to be most informative and fruitful.

I. Reports

The reports of investigating committees and commissions vary in size from a terse statement of a few pages to volumes running into hundreds of pages and accompanied by volumes of minutes of evidence, together with appendices containing experts' reports and factual or statistical material which has been collected by or presented to the investigating body to assist them in their deliberations. Sometimes a number of reports will be issued, each with its accompanying and relevant material, sometimes sub-committees will be given a section of the investigation and will make reports which they submit to the main body. The two investigations which published the largest amount of literature were the Royal Commission on Labour, 1892–94, with sixty-seven separately numbered papers, and the Royal Commission on the Poor Laws, 1909–10, with fifty-three separately numbered papers. But whether a report is small or very large, a great deal of trouble can be saved if before any attempt is made to read it solidly or to glean information from it, a little time is spent in examining the structure of the inquiry and its documentation.

(a) *Terms of Reference*

The authority of a committee and the scope of its investigations is determined by its terms of reference (in Scottish documents, remit) which are carefully drafted by the appointing authority. Though usually fairly short, they sometimes include a long series of specific questions to be examined. Their significance may lie not only in the problems included, but in the excluded matters which they are not authorized to investigate. A chairman may have to rule that a certain type of evidence offered is for that reason not admissible. An example is provided by the opening proceedings in the report of the Select Committee

32

on the *Port of London Bill*.[1] Occasionally the committee may feel that it cannot form a proper judgement on the matters put to it without investigating related questions, and the chairman may then be asked to inquire if the Minister will add to or extend the terms of reference. But sometimes limits are deliberately set to the field of inquiry in order to make the task manageable within a reasonable time, or because the Government of the day may wish to reserve some broad question, perhaps involving contentious political issues, for its own judgement.[2] The Labour Commission decided to keep to a fairly close interpretation of its specific terms of reference—the relations between employers and employed and the conditions of labour raised by recent disputes—and not to go into the social question generally, where the Minority thought the root of the matter was to be found. The terms of the Royal Commission on the *Delay in the Kings Bench Division*[3] led to the submission of a great amount of evidence on the radical reform of the whole judicial system, but the commission thought that neither Parliament nor public opinion would sanction such a revolution in order to remedy the complaints they were to consider.

(b) *Circumstances of Appointment*

A committee's approach to its problems, the emphasis in its interpretation of its terms of reference and the point of some of the questions to witnesses may often be more clearly understood if the circumstances in which the committee was appointed are known. These are sometimes given—though unfortunately not always when the information would be appropriate—in the report or its documents. The circumstances which led to the Commission on *Lunacy and Mental Disorder* were that the commission was set up after an action was brought in the High Court by a patient for wrongful certification, though the reference to the particular action is not given.[4] Or the circumstances of appointment may be found in the proceedings or in an appended paper. The chairman of the Royal Commission on *Police Powers and Procedure*[5] gave them in his opening statement on the first day of the oral evidence. Those for the Inter-Departmental Committee on *Physical Deterioration*,[6] which touched off so many investigations leading to the welfare services, are in Appendix I of Vol. I. The circumstances leading up to the Royal Commission on *Unemployment Insurance* are printed in the first day's

1   Chairman's ruling, p. 7; 1903 (288) viii.
2   See *State Purchase and Control of the Liquor Trade,* Cttees. Reps.; 1918 Cd.9042, xi.
3   1913 Cd.6761, xxx.
4   Min. of Health, Ann. Rep., p. 36; 1924 Cmd.2218, ix.
5   1928–29 Cmd.3297, ix.
6   Vol. 1, Rep. and App., p. 95; 1904 Cd.2175, xxxii.

evidence[7] given by the Ministry of Labour. Two spectacular cases were the Curtis Report on the *Care of Children*[8] which arose out of the O'-Neill case,[9] though this is not mentioned in the report, while the Crichel Down case and the issues it raised[10] formed part of the background to the appointment of the Franks Committee on *Administrative Tribunals*.

(c)   *Membership*

The course taken by an inquiry, the form, content, comprehensiveness or shortcomings of a report cannot fail to be greatly influenced by the personnel of the investigating body and their personal attitude as well as their special knowledge. The chairman is obviously in a key position; much depends on his capacity to draw his committee together, the guidance he gives it and his ability to secure an orderly and acceptable report. Though naturally not all chairmen have equally easy or equally difficult tasks or are equally able to meet the demands upon them, the practice of calling a report after the name of its chairman is a recognition of the fact. Obvious examples are the Haldane Committee on the *Machinery of Government*, the Gladstone Committee on *Prisons*, 1895–98, the Newcastle Commission on the *State of Popular Education*, 1861–62, the Macmillan Report on *Finance and Industry*, the Beveridge Report on *Social Insurance*, the Radcliffe Report on *The Working of the Monetary System* and the Robbins Report on *Higher Education*. Similar observations apply to individual commissioners or other persons making inquiries on behalf of the parent body. Chadwick's name is familiar; other examples are Tremenheere in the fields of education and poor law, Fox-Wilson in agriculture and Kay-Shuttleworth in education. For many years J. S. Haldane made scientific investigations for inquiries into the safety in mines. The influence of an individual member may be equally great, though it is less obvious and may have to be detected in the minutes of evidence. The contribution made by Keynes to the work of the Committee on *Finance and Industry* or by Stamp to that of the Colwyn Committee on *National Debt and Taxation*,[11] even if not perceived in the text of the report, can be gathered from the part each played in the cross-examination of witnesses.

But sometimes the political and other circumstances in which a

7   Mins. of evidence, first day, p. 7; 1931 Non-Parl. Min. of Labour.
8   1945–46 Cmd.6922, x.
9   Report by Sir W. Monckton on the circumstances which led to the boarding out of Dennis and Terence O'Neill at Bank Farm, Minsterley; 1944–45 Cmd.6636, iv.
10   *Disposal of Land at Crichel Down;* 1953–54 Cmd.9176, xi; and Report of a Committee *to consider whether certain civil servants should be transferred to other duties;* 1953–54 Cmd.9220, x. See *Breviate III*, p. 32.
11   1927 Cmd.2800, xi.

committee is set up may influence the selection of the persons appointed to it, so that despite the theory that they should be people of experience in public affairs and at least open to conviction if not impartial, they may in fact be less individual persons than representatives of the set view of various bodies or interests. This was clearly the case with the Amulree Commission on *Licensing (England and Wales),*[12] where the points of view represented were so violently opposed that a really satisfactory agreed report was unlikely from the outset. There were not only majority and minority reports, but a number of reservations on substantial points. The Sankey Commission on the *Coal Industry*[13] had a very controversial problem to handle: the nationalization of the industry. In a matter so bitterly contested openminded persons of public influence were not easy to find, but the expedient of adding members whose views on the main issue were already decided could not lead to an agreed report. One of them, Sidney Webb, gave evidence in favour of the principle upon which he was appointed to give judgement. The critical question was what conclusion its very able chairman would come to; he presented a report not signed by the others. The commission was not therefore valueless, for its hearings as well as its report received great publicity, and there is no doubt that the public was better informed of the facts and the principles involved than it would have been by any other process.

(d) *The Structure of the Report*

The key to understanding a report and therefore to an easy and efficient mastery of it may often be found by comparing the recommendations made with the terms of reference, since these show what the committee has made of its problems and how they have answered or not answered them. Large reports often end with a summary of the recommendations, accompanied by references to the relevant paragraphs of the text. But in some inquiries the recommendations are just embodied in the text as they are arrived at, and no summary of them is given. This form of the lay-out of a report seems to have been frequent among the departmental committees of the period 1900–17.

(e) *The Text of the Report*

The British people are fortunate in that generally the standards of orderliness, use of evidence and literary qualities in public documents are very high indeed; and as is, or ought to be expected from our long experience, many of those papers dealing with constitutional matters possess these characteristics to a high degree. For example, the report of the Inter-Imperial Relations Committee of the Imperial Conference,

12   1931–32 Cmd.3988, xi.
13   1919 Cmd.359, xi.

1926,[14] on the new relationship with the Dominions and of the Dominions with the Crown shows these qualities at a level worthy of a great state paper. They can be seen in a different way in the careful drafting of the report of the joint committee on the difficult problem raised by the Petition of the State of Western Australia, 1935.[15] The reports of the select committees of both Lords and Commons, since they now deal mainly with matters of limited scope, are necessarily short; but some are models of terse and skilful drafting. But in matters on which the House feels special concern, such as the working of the nationalized industries, the inquiries may be extended and vigorous and the reports substantial. Of the longer reports, those of the Samuel Commission on the *Coal Industry*,[16] of the Colwyn Committee on *National Debt and Taxation* or of the Macmillan Report on *Finance and Industry* are examples of work of this high order. But reports are not always so easy to handle. Sometimes the subject matter is very technical or the problem may be an intricate and complex one of economics, law and morals. In other cases the report is clearly the result of an attempt to secure general agreement between the members of the committee and bears the marks of divergencies of view and compromise. Sometimes a report may be extremely brief: the chairman's (Mr Justice Sankey's) report on the second stage of the *Coal Industry* inquiry which was concerned with the nationalization problem, is comprised in only ten pages, giving his conclusions on a great body of evidence which included the witnesses' answers to 28,000 questions. Two cases show the difficulties which are sometimes encountered. The first is that of the Committee on *Mental Deficiency* in 1929.[17] It was set up jointly by the Board of Education and the Board of Control. Each had its own problem on which it required information, and it is not always easy to understand or even to make consistent some of the statistics given, unless it is realized that in different parts of the inquiry the ground is being gone over from two different points of view. The second example is that of the Beveridge Report.[18] This masterly document, written by an experienced hand, needs close attention because, in effect, it is written in three layers or at three levels, Part I giving a short statement and summary, while Parts II and V set out general principles and proposals in different degrees of detail. Each 'level' could perhaps be read separately; indeed, they were no doubt aimed at the different audiences which would have to consider the plan.

14 Imperial Conference, 1926, Summary of Proceedings; 1926 Cmd.2768, xi.
15 1934–35 (88) vi.
16 1926 Cmd.2600, xiv.
17 1929 Non-Parl. Bd. of Education and Bd. of Control.
18 *Social Insurance and Allied Services;* 1942–43 Cmd.6404, vi.

(f)   *Majority and Minority Reports, Reservations and Dissents*

Sometimes the only way in which a chairman can get his committee to make an agreed report covering most of the ground is to arrange that individual members may attach reservations or dissents from particular recommendations or from some principle embodied in it or, occasionally, on the interpretation which has been placed on the terms of reference. But the disagreements may be too severe for this, and in that case there may be one or more minority reports signed by several members or even by one member only. It does not do to assume that the majority report, or according to one's temperament, the minority report, is more worthy of attention. Sometimes it is the majority report that has most influenced legislation, sometimes the minority; and on occasion both have been ignored. There are some famous minority reports. Among them is the 'Third Dissent' to the report of the Royal Commission on *Trade Unions, 1867–69,* signed by Lord Lichfield, Thomas Hughes and Frederic Harrison, and the 'Statement' signed by the two last named, which argued with understanding and ability the case for trade union legalization. The minority report on the Poor Laws, signed by four members, needs scarcely to be mentioned. Not only was it an able and well-documented report, the product of a coherent social philosophy, but as Mrs Webb's *Our Partnership* shows, it was 'put across' to the public by a vigorous and skilful campaign. Yet in practical recommendations many of its conclusions tallied with those of the majority, and there was a great deal of common ground between them. As we have seen, the report of the chairman of the Sankey Commission was signed only by himself; and in retrospect it is clear that the minority report of Sir Arthur Duckham, in its insistence on regional decentralization, was more far-sighted than the controversialists of the time admitted. Another example of a far-sighted minority report was that of Balfour of Burleigh, of the Royal Commission on *Local Taxation,* 1899–1903,[19] for in it he made separate recommendations for alleviating inequalities of local rates by the use of a formula for the distribution of grants which took account of the size of population, ability to pay and needs, and anticipated the later proposals of 1928–29. In the field of inquiries into agriculture, the minority report by Macgregor, a member of the *Agricultural Tribunal of Investigation,*[20] is noteworthy for the radical treatment of the subject. Other notable examples were the Selwyn Lloyd minority report on *Broadcasting* (1951) and the long and closely argued memorandum of dissent by Kaldor, Bullock and Woodcock, from the majority report on *Taxation of Profits and Income* (1955). Some reservations, such as Simey's to the Fulton Report on the *Civil Service* (1968), contain points of substance.

19   1901 Cd.638, xxiv.
20   1923 Cmd.1842, ix.

How to Use Them

The report of a select committee is a report of the committee as a whole; there are no minority reports. But the record of proceedings which accompany the report itself will contain the text of the draft proposed by the chairman for discussion, together with any amendments, and the names of proposers, seconders and a record of the voting. The proceedings are often enlightening. Those of the select committee on what were called the 'Marconi Scandals' (1912/13–1913) contain a draft chairman's report and two other main drafts. A comparison of the report as adopted with that of the draft and amendments proposed by Mr Falconer will show how much that member contributed to the final text.[21] The Committee on the *Luxury Duty, 1918,*[22] had many disagreements; the draft report prepared by Mr Vernon Harcourt was at once critical and constructive, but highly entertaining; perhaps it was the combination of shrewd sense with slight irreverence which led to its not being adopted.

The enlightenment to be obtained by comparing the majority and minority reports, or draft and final reports of a committee can also be gained by a glance at earlier reports on the same topic, not only for their historical interest, but for the practical one of seeing why it is that the problem comes up for discussion repeatedly. It is often the case that a recommendation of an earlier committee is repeated by subsequent inquiries and that an earlier proposal which seemed unimportant and was ignored is seen by a later committee to be a vital one.

(g) *Evidence*

The question is sometimes asked, 'Why bother with the evidence taken by the committee? It is the report and its conclusions which affect policy.' To this there are two answers. First, no matter how experienced and impartial they may be, the members of a committee come to their task of inquiry no doubt with open, but certainly not blank minds; they bring to it the pattern of ideas related to their time and derived from their experience, and the more active they have been in public affairs the more likely they are to have some firmly held principles. The report is not just summarized evidence, but evidence as interpreted by the committee. In weighing a report therefore, a distinction must be made between the evidence upon which it is based and what the members of the committee have contributed to it. There are cases of reports which seem, because of the strength of view of their authors, to go beyond the evidence. It has been said that the report on *Municipal Corporations, 1835,* was a case of this kind.[23] Certainly there have been examples where

21   1913 (152) vii.
22   1918 (101) iv.
23   Sidney and Beatrice Webb, *English Local Government: The Manor and the Borough, Part Two* (London 1908), pp. 721–22.

some of the conclusions seem contrary to the evidence. Secondly, evidence may be important quite apart from the report. That taken by the early nineteenth century committees contains information which has been invaluable to scholars who were not studying the particular problem under review by the committee, but were interested in other questions.[24]

(i) *Oral Evidence*. The evidence presented may consist of both oral evidence and of memoranda and statistical tables, etc. The method of inquiry by formal hearings, of 'question and answer', was a natural one in the early years of the nineteenth century when investigations were made by committees of the House, and had its own vivid effectiveness when the victims of the new social conditions, little factory children and later sweated workers, came before the House in person. Indeed, as methods of social research were rudimentary and there were few skilled investigators, it was sometimes the only effective method available. When in the absence of a responsible central department, the Commission of 1834 on the Poor Laws tried to remedy the complete ignorance of what was going on in the thousands of parishes throughout the country by appointing travelling assistant commissioners, it encountered difficulties in finding fit persons, as the varied quality of the reports confirms. The use by Royal Commissions of these traditional methods of inquiry sometimes led to the production of many massive volumes of oral evidence, as in the Commission on Depression of Trade and Industry, the Labour Commission, Poor Law Inquiry (1905–09) and some of the great nineteenth-century commissions on education. The sheer bulk of it began to raise questions on whether a good deal was merely repetitive or uninformed opinion and the use of personal examination of witnesses excessive and undiscriminating. It must have been extremely difficult for members of these commissions to master all the evidence—particularly for the Labour Commission, even though aided by ample digests of it and though many of its members were able and were distinguished in their respective professions. But it also seemed to underrate the alternative which the development of the social sciences now offered, of special inquiries by expert investigators, which might have been more productive.[25] Nevertheless, formal hearings continue

24 A classic example is the evidence of Viscount Haldane before the Sankey Commission on the problem of organizing and training a civil service to control a nationalized industry; it remains an invaluable text on the problems of public administration involved.

25 These important questions were raised sharply over the report of the Labour Commission. For the views of some of the participants in the discussion, see P. Ford, *Social Theory and Social Practice* (Shannon 1969), pp. 69–71, especially the sources referred to in footnotes 55–57 and 61. On oral and informal evidence see also *Poor Laws*, R. Com. Maj. Rep., par. 24; 1909 Cd.4499, xxxvii; *Taxation of Profits and Income*, R. Com. Final Rep., p. 3; 1955–56 Cmd.9474, xxvii.

to have their place, not only because in a democracy people will insist on opportunities of giving their point of view, but because hearings are a means of establishing a sequence of events, tapping personal and group experience, securing assessments of policy and discussing principles. These points emerge clearly from the inquiries into the Crichel Down case, the Radcliffe Committee on the *Monetary System,* the Morton Commission on *Marriage and Divorce,* the Franks Committee on *Administrative Tribunals* and the Redcliffe-Maud Commission on *Local Government in England.*

Sometimes oral evidence can be not only important, but decisive. Malthus's evidence to the Committee on *Emigration*[26] is a notable example. The conclusions of the Colwyn Committee on *National Debt and Taxation*[27] were greatly influenced by the arguments of Mr W. H. Coates, Director of Intelligence, Inland Revenue, as set forth both in the memorandum he presented and in his two days' cross-examination. The statements made by highly placed government officials, often early in the hearings of a committee, are generally first-class guides to the administrative, legal or other aspects of the problem the committee have before it. The evidence of Mr I. G. Gibbon before the Royal Commission on Local Government[28] was not only weighty, but remains a mine of information. The memoranda submitted to the Barlow Commission on the *Distribution of the Industrial Population*[29] by the Board of Trade (evidence, third and fourth days) and the Ministry of Labour (evidence, tenth and eleventh days) and the examinations based upon them were not only basic documents for the understanding of the problem the commission had in hand, but remain invaluable evidence raising questions of principle and providing carefully collected data. Certainly the impression and conviction produced by the evidence of the trade union leaders Applegarth, Allan, Guile, Coulson, and Potter before the Royal Commission on *Organization and Rules of Trade Unions and Other Associations,* 1867–69, led to a more understanding and favourable report when the feelings produced by the Manchester and Sheffield outrages might have brought about a very different result. A researcher who reads the evidence given by William Temple, J. Maynard Keynes and Josiah Stamp before the Royal Commission on *Lotteries and Betting*[30] will not be disappointed. Often the evidence presents a vivid picture of personalities, as in the hearings of Keir Hardie and Ramsay Macdonald before the Committee on the *Preservation of Order at Public*

26 1826–27 (88, 237, 550) v.
27 1927 Cmd.2800, xi.
28 Mins. of ev. Part I; 1923 Non-Parl. Min. of Health.
29 Mins. of ev., Third and fourth days; 1937 Non-Parl.; tenth and eleventh days; 1938 Non-Parl.
30 Mins. of ev.; 1932, 1933, Non-Parl.

Meetings,[31] or of clashes of personality such as that between Havelock Wilson of the Seamen's Union and Mr Walter Runciman, at the Committee on *The Mercantile Marine,*[32] or between Alfred Marshall as a commissioner cross-examining Sidney Webb as a witness before the Labour Commission.[33]

There are clearly great difficulties in handling the bulk of evidence provided by some of the great inquiries such as those named, since it is not always possible to go over it all. Apart from 'sample reading', there are two leads into it. It was the practice during the nineteenth century and particularly between 1900 and 1911 for reports to be issued with wide margins in which were printed marginal references to the relevant answers in the evidence. This practice, however, was ended on grounds of economy.[34] Some reports, either in appendices or on the contents pages to volumes of evidence, give the list of witnesses and often the body they represent or their professional or other qualifications for submitting evidence. Unfortunately the Royal Commission on *Local Government in England* broke a long and useful tradition by not stating in what capacity private individuals were acting when they sent in their written evidence.

(ii)   *Memoranda.* Written evidence varies according to the nature of the inquiry. At one end of the scale are the reports by Beveridge on the *Social Insurance and Allied Services*[35] and by the Royal Commission on *Population,*[36] neither of which issued any oral evidence. The appendix volumes of the former consisted entirely of memoranda, etc., submitted by various bodies. The Commission on *Population* set up three committees—economic, statistical and biological and medical—and it is the inquiries of these committees which formed the real work and evidence. Evidence other than hearings may also be invaluable as a source of information because it has been specially prepared by departments or experts. The memoranda by the Clerk of the House appended to the report of the Select Committee on *Witnesses*[37] and those by Mrs Sidney Webb, C. S. Loch, Professor Smart and Charles Booth, who were themselves members of the Royal Commission on the *Poor Laws,*[38]

31   Mins. of ev., pp. 56–63; 1909 Cd.4674, xxxvi.
32   qq. 16,777–16,830; 1903 Cd.1608, lxii.
33   Royal Commission on *Labour,* Evidence before the commission sitting as a whole, eighth and ninth days; 1893–94 C.7063–1, xxxix, Pt. I. The Select Committee of 1837 on the *Poor Law Amendment Act* asked Chadwick to compare his hotel bill of 18s to 20s a day with the 6s a week he advocated for poor relief; 1837 (131) xvii, Pt. I.
34   *Swine Fever,* Dept. Cttee. Rep., par. 65; 1911 Cd.5671, ix.
35   1942–43 Cmd.6404, vi.
36   1948–49 Cmd.7695, xix.
37   1934–35 (84) vi.
38   1909 Cd.4499, xxxviii.

are good examples of different types. The Select Committee on the *Increases of Wealth (War)*[39] was unable to get much further than to conclude that a tax on such wealth was practicable, but the memoranda prepared by the Board of Inland Revenue remain good papers on the problems and possibilities of taxing increases of capital. As the methods of social inquiry developed, in order to determine vital quantities or to test hypotheses based on numerical assumptions, the examination of witnesses for their opinions could be supplemented or replaced by statistical sampling methods. Early examples are the special *Investigation into the Incidence of Mental Deficiency in Six Areas* by Dr E. O. Lewis undertaken for the Committee on *Mental Deficiency, 1929,*[40] and the inquiry into what happened in sample areas to men who had been disallowed insurance benefit, made for the Royal Commission on *Unemployment Insurance, 1931–32.*[41] Following their use during the Second World War, there was an accelerated development of statistical methods and of their application to various fields of policy—to rail transport in the Beeching Report and to road transport in the Buchanan Report, while for the Robbins Committee reliable estimates of the number of young people capable of higher education were vital. And when we advanced to endeavours to plan or control the economy as a whole, many reports on the problem consisted entirely of elaborate and statistical argument produced by team research.

Sometimes decisive evidence consists of special inquiries undertaken at the request of the commission or committee itself. The Royal Commission on the *Press* (1949)[42] initiated an original and notable inquiry by appointing a team of research workers to examine the treatment by the press of selected topics and how far this was coloured or inaccurate. A series of special research papers was prepared for the Donovan Commission on *Trade Unions and Employers' Associations*[43] e.g., on the role of shop stewards and on overtime working in Britain, and for the Commission on *Local Government in England,* e.g. Local Government in South-East England and on the Inner London Education Authority.[44]

II. Bills and Acts

Of the hundreds of bills which come before Parliament only a small proportion ever reach the statute book. Of those which do become acts of Parliament a large proportion have been before Parliament in many forms and at different times, sometimes with intervals of many years

39   1920 (102) vii, and 1920 Cmd.594, xxvii.
40   1929 Non-Parl. Bd. of Education and Bd. of Control.
41   1931–32 Cmd. 4185, xiii.
42   1948–49 Cmd.7700, xx.
43   Research Papers 1–11; 1966–68 Non-Parl.
44   Research Studies 1–10; 1967–69 Non-Parl.

between them, before it is decided, for example, that the change is needed or the time is ripe, or that the law on a subject should be codified or consolidated. A researcher who is tracing the development of some piece of legislation in detail must necessarily make a study of the clauses and schedules of the relevant bills which led up to the climax of the act itself. But even for others less interested in details of this kind, the finding of the bill or bills may give a lead to the debates, to entries in the Journals, reports, etc. But bills also provide two other sorts of information. The actual clauses of Tudor acts of Parliament were often preceded by long preambles stating the reasons for the intended effects of the legislation (as in the Statute of Artificers, 1563, and the Poor Law Act, 1601). At the present time such preambles are not often incorporated in public bills, the long title being regarded as sufficient. But they are still used in bills of great constitutional importance, such as the Parliament Bill, 1911, or the Statute of Westminster, 1931, or in bills affecting international agreements. Occasionally the words setting out the aims of legislation have been incorporated with the short enacting formula which precedes the actual clauses, as in the Ottawa Agreement Bill, 1932. Next, a short explanatory memorandum, setting out the contents and objects of the bill in non-technical language or explaining its chief financial clauses and implication is often printed with the bill, or in a separate memorandum presented with it. The Coal Industry Nationalization Bill, 1945, the Transport Bill, 1946, the Housebuilding (Protection of Purchasers) Bill, 1965–66, and the Land Commission Bill, are examples of the former; the financial memoranda are printed with the National Insurance Bill, 1965–66, and the Agriculture Bill, 1946, but the explanatory memoranda are issued as separate Command papers. And generally a list of bills in any period indicates the problems which were in the minds of the public or a group of Members of Parliament and were being brought to the notice of the legislature as needing its attention. It is obvious that not only detailed amendments, but important changes of principle of significance for a problem under discussion, may be brought out by a comparison of a bill as introduced with its final form when it has received Royal Assent and has taken its place in the bound volumes of Public General Acts for the session. The action a government takes on the recommendation of a committee or commission may, however, not involve legislation but only administrative action. The steps proposed may be announced in the House, in which case the *Debates* should be searched, or set out in a circular, which may be listed in the Annual Catalogue.

The review we have made of the kind of material to be found in the papers and the ways in which it can be discovered and handled will indicate how much can be gained from an efficient and understanding study of them. This had been perceived by Henry Taylor, who in his *The Statesman*, published in 1836, gave his prescription for the training of a student aiming at a 'civil career'. The minutes of evidence of a parliamentary committee should be laid before him without their report. He was to be required 'to report upon that evidence himself exhibiting 1st. The material facts of the case as drawn from the evidence; 2d. The various views and opinions which have been or might be adopted in the matter; 3d. The conclusions of his *own* judgement, with his reasons; 4th. If he concludes for legislation, a draft of the law by which he would execute his purpose; 5th. A draft of the speech with which he would introduce his proposed law to the notice of the legislature.' A severe programme indeed, but one implying both the imaginative and critical attitude with which parliamentary papers can well be approached. For he said, discussing the value of this kind of study as compared with 'general history', 'Lord Strafford's despatches and Clarendon's state papers will be studied with more profit to a statesman than any history of the reign of Charles I, and it is the materials of history rather than the histories themselves,' which are of value to the young prospective statesman.

Special Collections of Papers and the Story of the Indexes

Including Notes on the Work of Abbot and the Hansards

In the first half of the nineteenth century Parliament ordered the preparation and printing of several collections of parliamentary papers and of so large a number and variety of indexes that it is difficult from the reading of a list to understand the relations between them. The history of this activity shows that the indexes fall into a clear and intelligible pattern. There are three distinct kinds of indexes to parliamentary papers—the indexes to collections of papers classified in subject order, the alphabetical indexes (bound in subject groups) to individual papers and the general alphabetical indexes to the sessional bound sets. The list below analyses these three different groups.

This large and impressive body of literature, published almost wholly before 1850, is an indication of that concern and generosity of Parliament which made possible the preservation and accessibility of its papers. The publication at irregular dates of the general alphabetical indexes occurred when a further accumulation of papers made Parliament aware of the need for the consolidation of the sessional indexes. 'Every seven years' vaguely influenced the decision to print, but it was not until 1879 that their publication settled down to what became the decennial pattern which, but for the interruption of the 1914–18 and the 1939–45 wars, has continued up to the present time. But the inconvenience caused by a periodic accumulation of sessional papers was only one factor influencing the minds of those concerned with this great experimental period of index making.

The work was largely the result of the co-operative efforts of a group of able men. At the beginning of the century the Speaker, the Clerk and the Printer shared an onerous responsibility for the papers. In 1818 the first Librarian was appointed, and in 1831 it was proposed at a select committee

> that at the commencement of each Session Mr Speaker should name a Standing Committee of five including himself, to whose direction should be referred all matters relating to the Library, the patronage to remain where it now is.[1]

---

1 *The Present State of the Library of the House of Commons*, Sel. Cttee. Rep., p. 10; 1831–32 (600) v.

Appendix I

This committee issued eleven reports between the years 1834 and 1857,[2] and it is from these that we trace much of the progress of the indexing of the papers. In this way work began to devolve on a larger number of people who eventually guided the pattern of activity. The Speakers for half a century gave their sympathetic sponsorship to the experiments. Henry Addington (1789–1801) urged Charles Abbot (1802–17) to give his attention to the papers. Abbot, with that passion for order which had already made him distinguished in so many fields, hardly needed this encouragement. John Rickman worked with Abbot as his secretary, and later as Clerk-Assistant to the House (1814–40); he became responsible for the indexing of the Journals, and gave his expert attention to directing and initiating work on the papers.[3]

But perhaps it is true to say that the greatest contribution to the indexing of the papers was made by Luke and Luke Graves Hansard. These two men, father and third son, were personally responsible for the printing, distribution and care of the papers from 1796 to approximately 1841. They were not only craftsmen of the highest repute, but in the course of their work as keepers and distributors of the papers they developed an academic interest in their contents as well as their use, and were stimulated to exercise personal initiative in making them accessible. Luke Graves Hansard's creative work went on almost up to his death in 1841, in spite of the fact that for years before his end he had been harassed by family disagreements in the printing business, by the growing challenge both inside and outside the House to the 'traditional craftsman' methods of printing by a private firm and by the result of the *Stockdale* v. *Hansard* case, which played havoc with his fortunes and damaged his health. For although the question of parliamentary privilege was involved, Parliament left him to take the financial strain of an action for libel in a parliamentary paper which he had been ordered to print and put on sale. When Luke Graves Hansard died the experimental period of index making in the nineteenth century was almost at an end.

The major decisions on the printing of indexes and on making special classifications of the papers other than the bound sets of sessional papers were made by three select committees.[4] But the story really begins in 1767 when Parliament for the first time voted large sums for the reprinting of a number of sessional papers. In the *Journal* (vol. 31, p. 412) there is the following entry:

2 *Select List, 1833–1899*, p. 6.
3 Ford, *Luke Graves Hansard's Diary, 1814–1841*.
4 *The State of the Printed Journals, General Indexes, and Volumes of Printed Reports*, Sel. Cttee. Rep.; Journals 1803, vol. 58, p. 653. *Committee Rooms and Printed Papers*, Sel. Cttee., Second and Third Reps.; 1825 (515, 516) v. *The Present State and Future Management of the Library and the State and Condition of the Printed Reports and other Papers presented to the House*, Sel. Cttee. Rep.; 1831–32 (600) v.

Ordered that one thousand five hundred copies of the several Reports from Committees of this House, which have been printed by Order of the House, and are not inserted in the said Journals, be reprinted, by the appointment and under the direction of Thomas Tyrwhitt, Esquire, Clerk of this House . . . be reprinted by such person, or persons, as shall be licensed by Mr Speaker and that no other person do presume to print the same.

The cost of this reprinting is not shown separately, but is included with other printing ordered at the same time. The total inclusive sum voted was £5,000. In 1773 a similar entry is found in the *Journal* (vol. 34, p. 385):

Ordered that one thousand five hundred copies of the several Reports from Committees of this House . . . be reprinted . . .

Again the figure is an inclusive one, this time being £7,500. The reports printed at this date were bound in four volumes double folio and form the first bound collection.

The next entry in the Journals is in 1803 (vol. 58, p. 653) when Lord Glenbervie reports from the select committee 'appointed to inquire into the state and condition of the Printed Journals of this House, and General Indexes thereto, and also of the volumes of Printed Reports'.[5] Appendix I to this report gives a list of 'stock in hand' and for the reprints of the reports ordered in 1773 the entry is '4 Volumes . . . None'. The report runs:

That it may be proper to print eleven volumes of Reports, in addition to the four which have already been printed; together with a General Index to the whole fifteen volumes of which the series will then consist [p. 654]. . . . as there has never been but one impression of the four volumes of Reports, and that impression consisted of 1,500 copies . . . your Committee think that 1,750 copies of each volume of the proposed new selection should also be printed. The value and importance of the Reports contained in the four printed volumes, as well as those specified in the above arrangement is very generally known and admitted but the benefit to be derived from them will be greatly enhanced, if direction shall be given for the preparing and printing with them of a well digested Index of the whole [pp. 653–4].

For the first time we get an estimate of the costs of this printing separated from the general printing account.

For reprinting the four volumes of Reports, 1,200 copies of each volume, £5,000 . . . and for printing eleven new volumes of Reports; viz. from Vol. V. to Vol. XV . . . together with a General Index to the whole 15 volumes of Reports:— 1,750 copies of each volume £18,000.

5   Not included in the bound sessional sets.

Luke Hansard, who made the estimate and presented a plan for the arrangement of the papers in each volume, adds this in appendix 2, p. 655:

> ... the above may be completed in about seven years; and may cost something more, or something less, than the above estimated sums, according as there may be a fall, or rise, in Paper or in Labour.

This set of fifteen journal size (double folio) volumes and index is called the *First Series*. It is the work of Luke Hansard, and the index is important because it bears the stamp which marks all his and his son's later index work. In the preface he explains the principles of his alphabetical arrangement, and shows his awareness of the need for accessibility through a subject, as well as an alphabetical order. The table of contents indicates how his mind was working on the various problems of index making:

> I. Arrangement of the Reports from Committees of the House of Commons, forming the Series of Fifteen Volumes; 1715–1801. II. Analytical Table of the Subjects referred to in the General Index. III. A List of the Reports inserted in the Journals of the House of Commons, but which are *not* included in the Selection forming this Series; with an Abstract of their Subjects. IV. Principal Heads of Reference in the General Index. V. The General Index.

In 1807, four years after the decision was made to reprint the collection of papers which was to form the First Series, there appeared a *Catalogue of Papers Printed by Order of the House of Commons 1731–1800,* 1807 (reprinted H.M.S.O., 1954). This is the Abbot Catalogue to the Abbot Collection of bound volumes of papers. Abbot himself records his work on page 617 of the *Diary of Lord Colchester,* 1861. In a 'short memorandum of my services . . .' both before and during his Speakership, he states:

> During Speakership, 1802–1817. 1. Series of printed papers of House of Commons, for nearly the last 100 years collected, methodised, and made accessible to public use . . .

The official record of the work is in the evidence of Mr Whittam, Clerk of the Journals, before the select committee of 1825.[6] In reply to a question about records of papers before 1800 he said:

> ... the room called the warehouse, which extends from the front in Abingdon-street to Sir George Rose's house . . . is appropriated exclusively for the printed Journals and Indexes . . . in the room over

6   Second Rep., pp. 3, 4; 1825 (515) v.

that there are complete sets of printed papers, from the years 1731–1800, inclusive, and from the union to the present time; which by the direction of Lord Colchester, when Speaker, are kept in that house, and are inscribed on the first page of each book, to be deposited in the official house of the Clerk of the Journals . . .

Q. Of how many volumes do these before the Union consist?—There are one hundred and ten volumes of the papers before the Union;

Q. Are the old Parliamentary papers to which you have spoken separated into volumes? — Yes; they were separated under Lord Colchester's direction. There are four sets completed; one kept in the Speaker's Gallery, one sent to the British Museum, one deposited in the Clerk of the Journals room at the Journal Office, and the remaining one was directed to be kept by the Clerk for the use of the House. No doubt they are all so inscribed.

Q. These four sets were similarly divided? — Exactly.

Q. They are supposed to be very complete? — There is a collection made of every printed paper then which was extant[7] [pp. 3, 4].

We can imagine the stocks of papers[8] which would not be wanted quite so much when the First Series came into circulation, and Abbot directing that they should be made into sets. Four sets were to be bound and the rest 'tied into bundles'. The preface to the Abbot Catalogue refers to the 'volumes' and to the 'bundles on the shelves'. The papers in these sets are arranged in the same three groups—bills, reports, accounts and papers—as they are in the sessional papers which were bound for the first time in 1801.

The work of the committee of 1803 was carried further by the select committee of 1825 on *Committee Rooms and Printed Papers*[9] which made two major recommendations:

(i) *The Second Series.* The report runs as follows:

In obedience to the order of reference, your Committee have proceeded to inquire into the state of the Printed Reports and Papers presented to the House. Referring to the Report made by the Select Committee, appointed for a similar purpose in 1803, they directed an arrangement to be made of Select Reports, similar to that adopted

7 By 'complete' and 'extant' Whittam was presumably referring to those papers in the official warehouse. Some papers had passed into the possession of members, and others had been put on sale. The British Museum possesses many of these papers from private collections.
8 'The earliest paper in our store is 1731': L. G. Hansard, in Appendix 3, p. 79, of the report from the select committee; 1837 (286) xiii.
9 Third Report; 1825 (516) v.

in the collection of fifteen volumes already printed . . . This arrangement will be found in the Appendix . . . The same motives which
induced the House in 1803 to reprint a Selection of the Reports then
existing, appear to your Committee sufficient to warrant a continuation of the series. But as a very considerable number of copies of
these Reports are still preserved in warehouses, your Committee do
not feel themselves warranted at the present moment in recommending
to the House the commencement of such an undertaking [pp. 3, 4].

The first part of this extract is a recommendation for the continuation
of the series, the last sentence means that they did not recommend the
continuation in the form of a reprint of twenty-five years of sessional
papers. Hansard had been asked to prepare estimates similar to those
presented for the fifteen volumes, but when the committee realized that
1,750 copies of the proposed set would cost some £45,000, or if printed
in folio size, something like £90,000, they looked for alternative methods
for making a collection. They questioned Hansard as to stocks in hand
and asked him to present a list. Hansard said that to gauge the extent of
such a reprint he had already made up from the existing papers one
complete set of reports for such a *Second Series* or collection. If this could
be done for the existing papers, then the work could be enlarged. In
view of this the committee went on to recommend:

> The classification to which your Committee have referred, applies
> at present, except in a few instances, to Reports only. It has occurred
> to your Committee, that a similar classification might with much
> utility be adopted as to the Papers [p. 5].

This Second Series finally comprised 56 volumes of bills, 154 volumes
of reports and 152 volumes of accounts and other papers in subject
classification. Five sets were made up, one for the Speaker's library,
one for the library of the Treasury, one for the Duke of Wellington,
one for Sir Robert Peel and one for the library of the French deputies.[10]
The plan for the series which Hansard presented to the committee
shows that he was responsible for the subject classification and for the
index to the collection, which he called a *Classification of Parliamentary
Papers and a Breviate of their Contents, 1801–1826*. The following
extract from his diary for 1829 gives an account of this Breviate and the
help he got from Mr Rickman:

> Apr. 2—Completed the abstract of the contents of the Reports of
> Committees from 1801 to 1826, and likewise the synopsis of the Ar-
> rangement of Vols. of the Reports and Accounts. Sent the MS. to
> Mr Rickman, with a memoir explaining the whole, and reporting to
> the Speaker the completion of the directions of the committee on

10   *Present State of the Library*, q. 86; 1831–32 (600) v.

Printed Papers in 1825. This abstract has been the work of many years; but it may not be thought proper to adopt it as a Parliamentary Paper—will [it] be allowable that it should speak of their contents in any other words than their own? Yet it is only an *Index raisonné*. I have my doubts whether it will be adopted; but having done it, I thought it would be well to let it be seen, as showing the attention bestowed on the Parliamentary Papers.

May 9.—Recd. a letter from Mr Rickman with a pf. of my introductory remarks and memoir. Says the Speaker is pleased with the general appearance, but has not yet had time to consider it. Mr Rickman has made many corrections and improvements; which I am glad of; because it is favourable to be thought worth mending.

May 23.—Mr Rickman has sent back the MS. volume, with a strip of paper on which is written 'that he will explain what is to be done with it'.

May 25.—Mr Rickman sent a letter explaining that the Speaker has shown the MS. to the Chancellor of the Exchequer and Mr Dawson, with his recommendation that it shd. be printed; which those gentlemen approved of. It is to be done during the recess carefully *for hurry would spoil such a work;* and a covering order will be given next Sessn. as in the case of the Genl. Index. The Index and this work, will show that the printer does not confine himself to the mechanical part of his duties, but is attentive to the intellectual also.

(ii) *A General Alphabetical Index.* The committee[11] also concerned itself with access to the sessional bound sets. They questioned L. G. Hansard:

Q. Have you taken any steps to combine those Sessional Indexes into one?—Certainly; we have for some length of time combined them, for the general use of our establishment, in order to facilitate the references to the Papers as wanted; we have them combined from 1801 to 1806, and from 1807 to 1812 and from 1813 to 1818, forming a complete general index to all the Papers then printed.

Q. Could there be much difficulty in making one General Index to all the Papers printed from the Union to the present time?—No, I should think not.

Hansard completed this first *General (Alphabetical) Index 1801–1826* at the same time as he completed the subject 'Classification and Breviate', and he suggested that the two volumes could be bound together to form 'one volume of Helps to Consultors of the Papers'.

The story repeats itself again at the select committee in 1831–32[12] when the same discussions took place over the need for an extension of

11 *Committee Rooms and Printed Papers*, pp. 7, 8; 1825 (516) v.
12 *Present State of the Library;* 1831–32 (600) v.

the subject classification and for more indexes. This committee recommended that there should be (1) a reprinted alphabetical index, extended up to 1832; (2) a Third Series of classified papers; (3) a general index to the series, and (4) a set of alphabetical indexes to individual papers. The following extracts from the minutes of evidence show that many of the suggestions were made by L. G. Hansard:

Q. 83. The classification of Parliamentary Reports, . . . now in your hand, was compiled, the Committee understand, in consequence of a recommendation of the Committee which sat in the year 1825, by you or by your Firm?—By myself, under my Father's directions.

Q. 84. Have you formed any plan for continuing such classification? —It has occurred to me that if the Committee should think proper to sanction the re-printing of the General Index to the Sessional Papers from 1801 to 1826, that it would be very desirable to continue the classification of the Papers from 1826 up to the present time, upon a plan similar to the classification laid down and recommended by the Committee of 1825.

Q. 85. Would you recommend that a second [third][13] series should be prepared up to the present time, for the use of the Library of the House?—It appears to me that that would be very advantageous; but the second [third] series might not of necessity be considered as a permanent series, but in case in the course of any given time (say seven years) when the Papers are accumulated to a greater extent, and another arrangement might be thought proper, then a permanent classification might be made to take the place of this temporary one, and thus become a permanent second [third] series. The present proposed arrangement, it appears to me, would be useful for the purpose of the Library.

Q. 93. Is the General Index to Sessional Papers one of those now out of print?—It is.

Q. 94. Has it to your knowledge and belief been found of great use, so far as you can infer from the frequency of applications?—Judging from applications made for it, I should conceive it has been found of considerable use. The experience that we have of its utility, is derived

13   In the evidence the series had been wrongly named. Hansard clears this in a letter to the chairman. 'It will be necessary to designate the arranged collections of Reports thus:—*First Series,* containing the Reports from 1701 to 1800, printed in 15 vols. large folio. *Second Series,* being the Reports arranged according to the direction of the Committee in 1825, from 1801 to 1826. *Third Series,* will be a continuation of the last up to 1832, which the Committee now recommend to be prepared as a temporary arrangement till the accumulation of seven years will make it of sufficient importance to be erected into a permanent collection. This will require an alteration in the wording of the Reports, as to the denomination of the *Series.*'

from the use which is made of it in forming selections of papers that are required either by Committees of the House, by Members, or by the Public Officers, and persons in Administration. When any subject is under discussion requiring information on any particular point, then applications are made to us for a selection of Papers, either individually or collectively, on those subjects. Without the means which that Index affords, we should find extreme difficulty and great delay in making the selections required; but with that we find the Papers with great facility, and are enabled to furnish them with accuracy and expedition.

Q. 100. In reference to that classification, is there any suggestion which you would desire to submit to the Committee with respect to the compilation of Indexes to any separate Reports, or any other Papers, progressively or otherwise?—This classification, and the Breviate of the contents of the volumes, were designed as a substitute for the want of Indexes to the particular Reports which are there enumerated. To the Reports which have been subsequently printed at least the most important of them, separate Indexes have been compiled during the progress of the Session, such as those on the State of Ireland, on East India Affairs, on the Poor Laws and several others. It has occurred to us, that it would be of very considerable advantage if separate Indexes were made to the Reports which are contained in the classification. This might be done progressively, and as opportunities occurred. These would then form one collection of Indexes, giving a complete mode of reference to all the most important matters which are contained in the Reports of this period.

We may now look at these projects in turn:

(i) *The General Alphabetical Index, 1801–1832.* The committee[14] had questioned Mr Vardon, the House of Commons librarian, on the possibility of enlarging this index to include the reports in the appendices of the papers:

Q. 51. Have you any Index to the Papers in the Appendices to Reports of Committees and Reports of Commissioners?—We have no Index at all to the Appendices of Reports, which I think is a great desideratum, for Committees are usually formed of those who understand the subject best, and they generally order those accounts to be laid before them which are of most value with reference to the subject referred to them; these Appendixes are bound up at the end of the Reports; they are at the time seen by the Members who form the Committee; afterwards there is an application made at the Library for what they wrongly, but naturally, call an Account or Paper laid

14   1831–32 (600) v.

before the House, for which we, having no reference at all to the Appendixes, can search in nothing but the Index to the Accounts and Papers where it is not; it is still insisted on that such a paper does exist, and then, after perhaps a very great deal of trouble, it is found out in an Appendix to a Report; but beyond that there is no means of reference whatever to these Papers . . .

This index was ordered to be printed in 1833. In the 'Explanation' on p. iv, L. G. Hansard throws light on the difficulties of indexing the reports in the Appendices. He confesses:

that the great extent of matter that would have required minute examination, in effecting such a purpose, rendered the desired addition to this index impracticable; but the recommendation has been adopted in the indexes to the Papers since 1832, where the references to such subjects are expressed '(in 747)' when comprised in other accounts and '(in App. to 612)' when inserted in Appendices to Reports. Thus the groundwork will be progressively formed, for any future General Index, with these and any such other improvements as time and experience suggests.

This promise was fulfilled in the general alphabetical indexes up to 1857, but it was not repeated after that time.[15] The extra work involved and the swollen size of the volumes must have acted as a deterrent to later compilers.

(ii) *The Third Series*. The work on the Third Series was delayed by the destruction of some of the material in the fire in 1834.[16] As late as 1845 we find the Library Committee[17] reporting that 171 volumes of the reports of committees from 1800 to 1837 had been 'classified in their respective subjects' and that 'we recommend that this should be done for Commissions.' The last volume covered reports on mines up to 1861. This set comprises 358 bound volumes of papers in subject order and is in the Library of the House of Commons.

(iii) *General Index to the Subject Classifications*. The recommendation to make an index to the three collections or series as envisaged by L. G. Hansard, who died in 1841, could not be carried out by him because the series was extended beyond 1837. There is, therefore, no index to the

15 This form of reference is used in the five general (alphabetical) indexes between 1832–57, but it was not carried forward to the 1852/53–1868/69 index. Although the numbers of entries decreased, it continued to appear in the sessional indexes up to 1889 when the reference to them in the 'Explanation' appeared for the last time.
16 Library of the House of Commons, Standing Cttee. Rep., p. 7; 1835 (104) xviii.
17 Library Committee, p. 3; 1845 (610) xii.

Third Series. What did happen was that a wide margin was provided in the *Index to the Reports from Select Committees* (1801–1845), where entries of the papers in the Third Series could be made at the side of the entries for the same papers in the bound sessional sets.[18] L. G. Hansard did, however, on his own initiative, provide a second *Catalogue of Parliamentary Reports and a Breviate of their Contents, 1696–1834* (I.U.P. reprint, 1970) sensing perhaps that the Third Series would continue indefinitely, and that in order to complete a classified index up to the date specified by the committee he must abandon the idea of indexing a completed Third Series. He made a classification using references to the Journals and the First Series for papers up to 1800 and the sessional bound sets for papers from 1801. He enters in his diary on 6 July 1836:

> The Catalogue of Parliamentary Reports from 1696–1834 which has cost me so much labour in compiling, was put into circulation. I hope under the blessing of providence it may do some good. I am thankful that I have had health and resolution to complete it—no trifling thing, considering it has been done during the trying period of the last four years.

(iv) *Alphabetical Indexes to the Contents of Individual Papers.* There are 191 separately numbered indexes, which are grouped together in a subject order corresponding to the volumes in the Third Series, but the references given for the individual papers are to the sessional bound sets. Some account of the progress made in the compilation of these indexes is given in the standing committee reports.[19]

The purposes of these indexes was first, to supply an index to each report which had been published without one; secondly, to group a set of indexes to be bound up with each subject volume of the Third Series where there were no indexes already; and thirdly, to provide one complete set of subject indexes to be used in conjunction with the sessional bound sets. Pages 58–61 show the numbered series within the whole set. Where these indexes have been bound with the sessional bound sets, the sessional references are given in the list; where they are not so bound the references are to the composite volume of subjects and to the groups of subjects.

The experimental period closes in 1852 with the consolidation of the five 'General Alphabetical Indexes' which had been published at irregular dates.[20] The Standing Committee of 1856[21] records that three

---

18   In the margin of the House of Commons copy of this index, entries have been written in for the papers contained in the Third Series.
19   See *Select List, 1833–1899*, p. 6.
20   See p. 62.
21   1856 (426) vii.

volumes of the 'General Alphabetical Index', 1800–1852, will be 'delivered to every member' asking for them. From 1852 to 1899 there is one 'General Alphabetical Index' for 1852–3 to 1868–9 and three decennial indexes. A fifty years' consolidated *General Alphabetical Index, 1852–1899,* was published, but it was not discovered until after it was presented that the reference numbers to the papers had not been given. There were no official subject classifications in the second half of the nineteenth nor in the twentieth century.

List of Collections of
Papers, Indexes and Catalogues

I. Bound collections of volumes of papers other than the bound sessional sets and their indexes and catalogues.

1731–1800	Abbot Collection	110 volumes of 'original separates'. Chronological index—*Catalogue of Papers, 1731–1800*. 1807; reprinted H.M.S.O., 1954.
1715–1801	First Series	15 volumes of reprinted papers (double folio). Index—16th volume.
1801–26	Second Series	Reports, 154 volumes. Accounts, 152 volumes. Bills, 56 volumes. Indexes—*Classification of Parliamentary Reports, and a Breviate of the Contents;* 1829 (81) iv. *General (Alphabetical) Index, 1801–26;* 1829 (49)—.
1801–61	Third Series	358 volumes in the House of Commons Library. No Index.

II. Subject catalogues and breviates.

	1715–1801	*General Index* to the First Series contains a subject classification.
1830 (81) iv	1801–26	*Classification of Parliamentary Reports, and a Breviate of their Contents:* likewise Tables of Arrangement in Volumes of the Accounts and other Papers and Bills, o.p. Feb., 1830. (Index to the Second Series.)
1834 (626) lii	1696–1834	*Catalogue and Breviate of Parliamentary Papers.* o.p. Aug., 1834; reprinted I.U.P., 1970.
(498–I) lii	1835–37	——Supplement.

III. Alphabetical indexes to the contents of individual papers bound in subject order.

There are three main series of indexes and some separately numbered ones. The following table shows first the three main series and secondly

57

Appendix I

an analysis of these series, with the separately numbered indexes inserted chronologically. (The small roman numbers indicate when an index is in the sessional bound set.)

1. Main Series.

1834 (626)   1   1801–34 Indexes to the Subject Matters of the Reports of the House of Commons. o.p. Aug., 1834. (Number on the document 626A).

1837 (498)   1   1801–34 ——Supplement (Revised Table of Contents).

1837 (498–II   Indexes to the Subject Matters of the to VIII)   Reports of the House of Commons. o.p. July, 1837.

1847 (710–I   Indexes to the Reports of Commission- to XVIII)   ers. o.p. Feb., 1847.

2. Analysis of the three series, with separately numbered indexes inserted chronologically.

1816   (51)   x   Military Inquiry. Coms. 1806–12.
1826–27   (281)   viii   Charities in England and Wales.
1834   (626)   1   *Indexes to the Subject Matters of the Reports of the House of Commons.* (Number on the document 626A.)
                           ——(626–I) Agriculture and Corn Trade, 1820–34.
                           ——(626–II) Colonies and Slavery, 1803–34.
                           ——(626–III) Emigration, 1826–27.
                           ——(626–IV) Poor, 1813–33.
                           ——(626–V) Poor in Ireland, 1819–30.
                           ——(626–VI) Brewing, Malting, Distillation, 1804–33.
                           ——(626–VII) Weights and Measures, 1814–34.
                           ——(626–VIII) Children employed in Factories, 1816–32.
                           ——(626–IX) Foreign Trade, 1820–24.
                           ——(626–X) Fisheries, 1803–33.
                           ——(626–XI) Salt, 1801–18.
1837   [84]   xxx   Excise Establishments, 1833–37.

Indexes to Reports of the House of Commons, 1801–34

On the cover of each volume	On each index in the volume	Sess. vol.	
1837 498–IV	498–I	not	Ecclesiastical, 1810–39.
,,	498–II	bound	Education, 1814–34.
498–II	498–III	lii	Civil List, 1801–33.
498–IV	498–IV	not bound	Finance, Public Accounts, 1807–29.
498–II (Cont.)	498–V	,,	Banking, Coinage, Currency, Exchange, 1804–32.
498–III	498–VI	,,	Parliament, Privilege, 1815–40.
,,	498–VII	,,	——, Members.
,,	498–VIII	,,	——, Elections.
,,	498–IX	,,	——, Proceedings.
,,	498–X	,,	——, Establishment, Printing.
,,	498–XI	,,	——, Library.
,,	498–XII	,,	——, Houses of Parliament, 1831–41.
,,	498–XIII	,,	——, Reform of Representation, 1830–32.
498–IV	498–XIV	,,	——, Municipal Reform, 1819–33.
498–II	498–XV	lii	——, State of Ireland, 1824–32.
498–II	498–XVI	not bound	Trade and Manufactures, 1802–35.
498–VII	498–XVI(2)	,,	Trade and Manufactures, 1801–32.
498–II	498–XVII	lii	Bread Assize, 1804–24.
,,	498–XVIII	lii	Medical, 1807–34.
498–IV	498–XIX	not	Debtor and Creditor, 1816–34.
498–V	498–XX	bound	Law and Law Courts, 1811–34.
,,	498–XXI	,,	Seditious Practices, 1812–18.
,,	498–XXII	,,	Annuities, Usury, etc., Friendly Societies, 1812–29.
,,	498–XXIII	,,	Commerce and Shipping—Shipwrecks, 1810–34.
,,	498–XXIV	,,	East India Affairs, 1805–32.
,,	498–XXV	,,	Steam Power, 1817–34.
498–VI	498–XXVI	,,	Arts and Literature, 1805–34.
,,	498–XXVII	,,	Woods, Forests and Land Revenues, 1829–34.
,,	498–XXVIII	,,	Public Offices, 1810–34.

1837	498–VII	498–XXIX	,,	Roads and Bridges and Harbours, 1803–30.
	,,	498–XXX	,,	Public Buildings, 1807–33.
	498–VI	498–XXXI	,,	Highways, Wheels and Carriages, 1806–33.
	498–VII	498–XXXII	,,	Local Improvements and Taxation, 1809–34.
	498–VIII	498–XXXIII	,,	Public Works, Ireland, 1809–34.
	,,	498–XXXIV	,,	Local Taxation, Ireland, 1815–34.
	498–VI	498–XXXV	,,	Crime, Police, Punishment, 1812–34.
	,,	498–XXXVI	,,	Prisons, Prison Discipline, 1811–26.
	498–VIII	498–XXXVII	,,	Army and Navy, 1805–33.
	,,	498–XXXVIII	,,	Population—Registration, 1830–33.
	,,	498–XXXIX	,,	Miscellaneous, 1808–34.
	,,	498–XL	,,	Parliament—Legislative Assemblies, 1826.
1840	(10)		xlii	Post Office and Postage, 1835–39.
1859 Sess. 2	(0.41)		not bound	Parliamentary Subjects, 1836–58.
	(0.41) Sess. 2		,,	East India, 1835–59.
1861	(0.41)		,,	Mines and Collieries, 1842–61.

Indexes to the Reports of the Commissioners

1840	(279)	xix Pt. II	Charities in England and Wales, 1819–40.
1845	(40)	xliii	Poor Law, Ireland, 1835–39.
	(643)	xlii	Education, Ireland, 1814–44.
1846	(673)	xli	Law Courts, 1810–45.
1847	(70)	lviii Pt. I	Public Accounts, 1800–33.
	(71)	lviii Pt. II	Roads and Bridges, 1800–46.
	(710–I)	lviii Pt. IV	Emigration, 1828–47.
1847	(710–I$_2$)	lviii Pt. IV	West Indies and Mauritius (Labour), 1832–47.
	(710–II)	lviii Pt. II	Railways, 1837–46.
1847	(710–III)	lviii Pt. III	Public Works (Ireland), 1810–46.
	(710–IV)	lviii Pt. IV	Colonies, 1812–40.

	(710–V)	lviii Pt. III	Shannon Navigation, 1832–47.
	(710–VI)	,,	East India, 1806–47.
	(710–VII)	,,	Exchequer Bills, 1811–42.
	(710–VIII)	not bound	Revenue Inquiry, 1822–34.
	(710–IX)	,,	Excise Inquiry, 1833–37.
	(710–X)	,,	Army, 1806–40.
	(710–XI)	,,	Naval Inquiry, 1803–06.
	(710–XII)	,,	Civil Affairs of the Navy, 1801–40.
	(710–XIII)	,,	Agriculture, 1801–43.
	(710–XIV)	,,	Handloom Weavers, 1839–41.
	(710–XV)	,,	Factories, 1833–41.
	(710–XVI)	,,	Customs, Excise, Stamps, Land Tax, 1810–44.
	(710–XVII)	,,	Fees, etc., Public Offices, 1806–37.
1854	(448)	lxviii	Docks, Harbours, etc., 1802–53.
	(448–I)	lxiv	Parliamentary Representation, 1832–54.
	(448–II)	lv	Poor Law, 1835–48.

IV. General Indexes.

1. *Chronological Index.*

| | | | 1731–1800 | Catalogue of Papers, 1807. (See Abbot Collection.) |

2. *General (Alphabetical) Indexes.*

			1715–1801	General Index. (See First Series, 1803.)
1829	(49)		1801–26	General Index. o.p. Feb. 1829.
1833	(737)	xl	1801–32	——o.p. Aug. 1833.
1840	(11)	xlix	1832–38	——o.p. Jan. 1840.
1845	(396–I)	xliv	1832–44	——o.p. June 1845.
1850	(698)	xlvii	1845–50	——o.p. Aug. 1850.
1857 Sess. I	(125)	xvii	1852/53–1857	——o.p. March 1857.
1862	(0.55)	lxv	1852/53–1861	——o.p. Aug. 1862.
1870	(469–II)	lxxi	1852/53–1868/69	——o.p. Aug. 1870.
1880	(140)	lxxxiii Pt. I	1870–1878/79	——o.p. March 1880.
1889	(354)	lxxxix	1880–89	General Index. Alphabetical Index. o.p. Aug. 1889.

1904	(368)	cxii	1890–99	——Alphabetical Index. o.p. Aug. 1904.
1911	(351)	civ	1900–09	——o.p. Dec. 1911.
1926	(169)	xxxi	1910–19	——o.p. Dec. 1926.
1930–31	(8)	xxxvii	1920–1928/29	——o.p. Nov. 1930.
1946–47	(1)	xxvii	1929–1943/44	——o.p. Nov. 1946.
1950–51	(175)	xxxiv	1944/45–1948/49	——o.p. April 1951.
1962–63	(96)	xxxix	1950–1958/59	——o.p. Jan. 1963.
1845	(396–II)	xlii	1800–45	Index to Report from Select Committees. o.p. June 1845.
1854	(0.8)	lxx	1801–52	General Index. Vol. I. Bills. o.p. Aug. 1853.
	(0.9)	lxx		——Vol. II. Reports of Select Committees. o.p. Aug. 1853.
				——Vol. III. Accounts and Papers, Reports of Commissioners, Estimates, etc., etc. o.p. Aug. 1853 (reprinted H.M.S.O., 1938).
			1852–99	General Alphabetical Index. o.p. Sept. 1909. (No paper numbers.)
			1900–49	General Index 1900 to 1948–49. H.M.S.O., 1960.

APPENDIX II

The Debates

Note on the Methods of Compilation, Accuracy and Style.

The Select Committee on *Parliamentary Debates,* 1893,[1] recommended that the proposed official version should be *substantially verbatim* and in the *first person.* This recommendation was the conclusion of a discussion which had taken place in many select committees in the nineteenth century, and had arisen as a result of criticism of the methods of compilation. This note sets out some of the evidence given to these committees on the methods of compilation, accuracy and style of the Debates.

Originally the Debates had been conceived by Cobbett, and then by Hansard, as part of a plan in which they were to be 'continued downwards' from a Parliamentary History. From 1803 to 1829, when the thirty-sixth, and last volume of the History was published, both projects were running simultaneously, and therefore the methods of compilation were somewhat the same: for the History, past records were used; for the Debates, current records.

The preface to the first volume of the History, published in 1806 and signed by Cobbett, describes his methods of compilation in the following manner:

... principally from the Records, the Rolls of Parliament, the Parliamentary or Constitutional History, and from the most reputable English Historians. From the Reign of Henry the Eighth inclusive, we have the additional aid of the Journals of the House of Lords; and from that of Edward the Sixth, that of the Journals of the House of Commons. Sir Simonds D'Ewes' Journal of Queen Elizabeth's Parliaments, has been diligently consulted, and the Debates of the House of Commons in the years 1620 and 1621, published from the Manuscript in the Library of the Queen's College, Oxford, have been carefully incorporated, under their respective dates. The State of the Peerage, and Lists of the Members of the House of Commons have, from time to time, been given: and at the close of the Parliamentary History of each reign, will be found Lists of the Public Acts passed; together with an account of the Taxes imposed, of the Supplies, of the State of the Revenue, and of the Value of Money in relation to the Price of Provisions.

Cobbett goes on to say that the history was intended to supersede other histories which were 'very scarce' or 'excessively voluminous' and cites them in the following order:

1   1893–94 (213) xiii.

Appendix II

'The Parliamentary or Constitutional History', in Twenty-four Volumes; the second, 'Sir Simonds D'Ewes's Journal of Queen Elizabeth's Parliaments'; the third, 'Proceedings and Debates of the House of Commons in 1620 and 1621, collected by a Member of that House, and published from his Original Manuscript in the Library of Queen's College, Oxford', in Two Volumes; the fourth, 'Chandler's and Timberland's Debates', in Twenty-two Volumes; the fifth, 'Debates of the House of Commons, from the year 1667 to the year 1694, collected by the Honourable Anchitell Grey, Esq., who was thirty years Member for the town of Derby', in Ten Volumes; the sixth, 'Almon's Debates', in twenty-four Volumes; and, the seventh, 'Debrett's Debates' in sixty-three Volumes.[2]

The first volume of the debates, for the year 1803, was published in 1804. Seventy-four years later, before the Select Committee on *Parliamentary Printing*,[3] T. C. Hansard, Junior, described the methods of compilation, accuracy, style and length of the Debates, as indicated by the following extracts:

1. *Compilation and Accuracy of the Debates*

    Q. 160. . . . Before [1833 when Hansard Senior died] the work was compiled by gentlemen of some literary importance from every source which was at that time available; newspapers, pamphlets, manuscripts, and other very miscellaneous sources.

    Q. 161.. . . . Never by the employment of reporters by Mr Hansard himself in the Reporters' Gallery?—That is my meaning.

After 1830 T. C. Hansard employed reporters on special occasions:

    Q. 164. When you speak of special arrangements and special reports asked for, by whom were they asked for?—By associations or individuals interested in particular subjects then before Parliament.

    Q. 167. What other means had you for ensuring the accuracy of the report which appeared under your name?—In the first instance, a staff of collators and revisers employed and paid by me. The reports so collated having been got into type, the proofs of the speeches were sent to almost every individual speaker, in slips, with a request that the proof slips should be returned at a proper time.

    Q. 194. There are some speeches which occur in Hansard with an asterisk affixed to them; what does that mean?—Those are speeches which are sent to me, and which I carefully examine myself. If I find that it has every appearance of being a *bone fide* report of the

2   *A Bibliography of Parliamentary Debates of Great Britain,* House of Commons Library, Document no. 2 (1956).
3   1878 (327) xvii.

The Debates

speech delivered, although it may evidently not be a verbal report—still, if I am satisfied that it is a *bona fide* report, I accept it; but I put the asterisk to signify that I publish it on the authority of the Member with my own ratification of it.

In 1878 the Treasury made a grant to T. C. Hansard to enable him to report more fully, for which purpose he engaged four full-time reporters.

Q. 252. The arrangement that you now have with the Government is to report specially four things: first, late Sittings after Midnight; then the proceedings in ordinary Committees; the proceedings in Committee of Supply; and the discussions on Private Bills 'by Order'? —Yes, those are the four points.

Q. 306. Do you consider that you have a kind of moral responsibility to the House of Commons to deal with speeches in the manner that you have described, and not to permit unfair alterations?—I consider that I have a moral duty to exercise that power.

Q. 317. Then is it the inference from what you state, that the fact of 'Hansard' being quoted in the House of Commons as almost an official publication arises from the fact, that it was almost the only publication which gave reports of the proceedings in the House of Commons on which Members could rely—I think so; the authority of 'Hansard' is not, and never has been in any sense official or authoritative; it has rested always upon the confidence placed in the character of those who conduct it.

Q. 448. You have never known any case in which a debate has been entirely omitted from 'Hansard'?—Yes, in early days.

Q. 449. I am speaking of a debate being purposely omitted; has there never been any pressure brought to bear upon 'Hansard', to omit a debate altogether?—Never. In answer to that question, I might say generally that I am treated, and always have been treated by Members, I may say, as a formidable person—I have never been asked to do what you refer to, and nobody seems to dare to ask me.

2. *Style of Debates*

Q. 347. I notice in looking over 'Hansard' that the general run of speeches are given in the third person, but some in the first; is that always the doing of the Member who corrects the speeches, or is there a difference made to certain Members by you?—There is no difference made to certain Members as such; no Member is entitled to ask or press me to report either in the first person or in the third; it depends upon the reporter.

Q. 348. And it is not always the result of the Member's own correction?—Never.

65

Q. 349. He does not transfer from the third to the first person?—Almost never.

Q. 350. There are many speeches that appear in your publication and occur in a debate which in the newspapers are given in the third person, but in yours in the first?—When they are derived from a source where the speech is given in the first person.

Q. 351. What source would that be?—The special reports for country newspapers and other sources in which the original is in the first person. But more frequently the report in the first person is the speech of some very important Member or Minister whose speech it is desirable to take at full length, and then it is more easy to take it in the first person than in the third.

3.   *Length of the Debates: Summary, Full or Verbatim?*

Q. 469. Have you compared the length of the present publication of 'Hansard' not in the present year, but up to this year, when the reports were furnished by collation of newspaper reports; have you ever made any comparison between the length of your reports and the fullest reports of the London papers?—I do not think I have.

Q. 470. They would probably not greatly exceed in length, would they, the reports of the fullest London papers?—Very much.

Q. 473. For that reason, then, should their reports exceed in length the reports in those papers?—My Manager informs me that he thinks that the excess of Hansard in past years over the reports of the London journals has been nearly one-half.

Q. 474. When you say the London journals, do you mean the average of the London journals, or the reports of the fullest of the London journals?—They vary so; one of the most important journals gives as a general rule very much longer reports than are given in the others.

Q. 477. Now, is it your opinion or not that the length of a report ought to depend, to a considerable extent, upon the quality of the speeches?—No; I do not know that any one in the office of Hansard is entitled to judge either of the importance of the Member who makes the speech, or of the importance of the subject to which it refers.

Q. 478. Would you apply the same rule to the newspaper or would you confine it to the official report?—It is universally applicable; I do not think there ought to be any difference.

Q. 479. Has it come within your knowledge that it is possible for a Member to make a very long speech and to repeat the same arguments very frequently, so that the Speaker of the House of Commons has called him to order on that account?—I have seen it, and heard it.

Q. 480. Do you think that when a man speaks for half-an-hour and repeats the same arguments repeatedly, and is called to order by the Speaker for such conduct, he should be reported at length, even in the official report?—If I answered that question without reserve, I might say that which Members when they come to read the report of the proceedings of the Committee might not like.

Q. 481. It is an important question for us to have your opinion upon?—I think there should be vested in the hands of the director of the reports a power to report in a more concentrated form those debates which take place in the House late at night, after 12 o'clock, which consists for the most part in repetition of arguments.

Q. 485. Would you not consider that there were a great many debates not of that character in which there is a great deal of surplusage?—That is the business of the House, not mine. If they permit it, it is my business to report it.

Q. 486. Would you consider that a full report of a debate of that character is equally satisfactory to the House—I would very willingly sift them, but I do not think it is my province to do so.

Q. 492. I want to ask you whether, so far as you know, any of those speeches were sent before they were actually made?—No, never; no such thing has ever occurred upon any occasion.

Hansard had been questioned on whether it would not be better to have official reporters, instead of relying on other sources for material, and the reply he gave expressed the principle which finally determined the length and composition of the Official Debates.

Q. 311. Have you found that there is a general desire for verbatim reporting, or for full and accurate reporting?—I think that while some enthusiasts go to verbatim reporting, the general opinion is for full and accurate reporting; the public do not require verbatim reports.

Q. 312. Then the official reports to which you refer would not be verbatim reports, but full and accurate reports?—They would be full and accurate, but they would not be verbatim in this respect, that certain duplications, and small matters which, as any gentleman in the House of Commons knows perfectly well, are not necessary to the argument or sense to be recorded, would be omitted; otherwise they should be verbatim.

Ten years later the matter came up again before the Select Committee on *Cost and Method of the Publication of the Debates and Proceedings*[4] because of the dissatisfaction felt over the disproportionate lengths of reporting speeches, etc., compared with those for which Hansard received a grant-in-aid, the cost of the Debates, and perhaps the most important point, the difficulty of understanding how one man could be responsible for the production of the Debates, especially when he had so small a staff compared with the sixteen reporters of *The Times*. The committee questioned Hansard on these points, and his replies were as follows:

4   1888 (284) x.

Q. 18. With whom at present do you consider the responsibility rests for the reports which are contained in Hansard's Debates?—With me entirely.

Q. 19. With you personally?—With me personally.

Q. 27. Do not you think that would cause some difficulty in producing very lengthened reports of debates in Parliament if every word that was uttered in either House were to be officially reported?—I am afraid the mass would be so overwhelming that the public in general would get very tired of Parliamentary institutions.

Q. 127. Did you ever hear of a speech being printed before it was delivered?—I have heard of such things, but I have never used them. I had one narrow escape, certainly, but was wise in time.

Q. 221. You have the report of an important speech taken from *The Times,* or any source you like, and you supply the member with a copy of his speech; he makes a considerable number of alterations; you look at it and sometimes decide that you will not accept his revision; now upon what grounds do you decide; is it by looking at the reports of *The Times* or other newspapers, and seeing whether those are really *bona fide* a more correct statement of what he said than the one which he has returned to you, or do you not approve of second thoughts being best because, as I should presume, most of those would be *bona fide* alterations?—If I think a speech has been unfairly corrected, I decline to use it.

Q. 222. But how do you arrive at that conclusion; that is what I cannot understand?—I look to the different authorities, and you can tell pretty well whether or not it is new matter which has been inserted.

Q. 223. You would not allow any new matter to be inserted unless it could be shown that it has been inserted in *The Times,* the *Standard,* or other principal newspapers?—Unless it could be supported by collateral authority.

Q. 224. Do you ever send back to gentlemen who send in these revises and ask them for such evidence?—No.

On the costs of producing the Debates more fully the evidence of Mr Digby Pigott, head of H.M.S.O., was decisive: in qq. 242, 243 he states that Mr Hansard had asked for £20,540 for what 'could be done, roughly, for £10,000'. The committee therefore recommended

> ... that a Report which might be described as an improved and amplified Hansard should be obtained; that public tenders should be invited for such a Report; that the Contractor should be allowed to procure his Report from any source he might choose, subject, however, to the condition that he should be required to keep reporters constantly present during the sitting of each House to take notes, which would supply any deficiencies or correct any errors in the Reports; that the Contractor should be allowed to exercise his own discretion as to the

fulness of the Reports given, subject only to the condition that no speech should be reported at less than one-third of its length as delivered; that the Debates in Committee of either House and Debates on Private Bills should be reported with the same fulness as Debates on public questions, without regard to the hour of the delivery of the speech; . . .

In effect this recommendation was for more 'Debates' for less money, and it cannot be said that subsequent events bore out the confidence of Mr Pigott and of the committee as to the cost of getting what they required in length, accuracy and speed. This is clear from the evidence given to the Select Committee on *Parliamentary Debates* four years later, in 1893.[5] It is not surprising, in view of the methods used to select contractors (Pigott, qq. 17–42) that several successive contractors had to be employed in the first ten years, that two went bankrupt[6] and that only after 1899 was it carried on steadily. Mr F. Hoole, one of Hansard's old reporters, gave some interesting evidence on the cost of proper service, and his estimate was fifty percent greater than the increased sum being demanded by the contractors (qq. 1123, 1130–1152). The contractors were less experienced and less independent than Hansard, so that extensive corrections of the reports of their speeches by members was not unknown (qq. 672–685, 1121, 1379–1381). And the form of the index changed with the contractor (qq. 1680–1683). The existing con-tractor (Eyre and Spottiswoode) took occasion to state the advantage of permanence and experience (qq. 399–401). The problem of which T. C. Hansard had complained in his evidence before the committee of 1888 and which that committee had failed to understand, was sum-marized by the 1893 committee:

> The question which first arises is that of the length and character of the Reports. There are three kinds of Reports which have to be considered. The first kind is the strictly verbatim Report, in which every word uttered is recorded, and which may, perhaps, be concisely described as a phonographic Report; the second is the full Report, which, though not strictly verbatim, is substantially the verbatim Report, with repetitions and redundancies omitted, and with obvious mistakes corrected, but which, on the other hand, leaves out nothing that adds to the meaning of the speech or illustrates the argument; the third is the condensed form of Report . . . the report to be adopted for the future should be of the second kind, i.e. should be a full report

---

5   1893–94 (213) xiii. It was apparently not part of H.M.S.O.'s duty to see that the quality of the reports (that is, as to length) were as required. See qq. 134–36, 277–80.
6   Mr Horatio Bottomley was secretary of one of them. For an account of these and of the ending of T. C. Hansard's connection with the debates, see J. C. Trewin and E. M. King, *Printer to the House* (London 1952), pp. 253–61.

of all speeches alike . . . that the Report should (as is usual now with a full Report) in all cases be in the first person. Reports in the third person, however complete, are open to the objection that they substitute a narrative for a speech, and the personality of the reporter for that of the speaker (pp. iii and iv, and T. P. O'Connor, q. 1717).

It was another fourteen years before recommendations were made that Parliament should itself take over the full responsibility of the reporting, printing and publication of the debates. The following extract from the Reports from the Select Committee on *Parliamentary Debates*[7] which made the recommendation shows how the matter was finally settled.

Your Committee are convinced that great dissatisfaction exists amongst Members of the House of Commons as to the present reporting of Debates, and that this dissatisfaction is justified. They are of opinion that the system of obtaining reports of Debates in the House of Commons by contract has not been a success for the following reasons:—(1) No system can be good under which it is to the interest of the contractor to lengthen or shorten his reports according to the terms he has received. Under the system of granting a subsidy of so much per volume it is to the advantage of the contractor to lengthen his reports and expand the printing if the terms he has received are good, and to shorten them if he has miscalculated and they are unremunerative. (2) It is unfair to Members that a contractor's reporter should be the judge—subject, of course, to the one-third limit of the contract—as to the length at which speeches should be reported, and such a system deprives the reported speeches of much of their historical value. (3) The contract system must tend to the employment of too few reporters, and has in fact had that effect, with the result that the present staff has been seriously overworked, and their work has naturally suffered. In the opinion of your Committee this overwork has been persistent, and in some cases very excessive, as, for example, this Session, when during the Debate on the Army Annual Bill the staff were on duty for more than 20 consecutive hours. (4) A contract like the present one, which permits the contractor to obtain his reports from any source, provided he has a reporter always present in the House, leads largely to the use of newspaper cuttings in the making up of the reports, and, even although the contractor's reporters check these cuttings with their own notes, must tend to destroy the independence of the final version of speeches.

Your Committee therefore condemn the system of obtaining the reports by contract and recommend that the House of Commons should set up a reporting staff of its own.[8]

7   1907 (239) vii.
8   Ibid., pars. 7, 8.

Bibliographical Aids

I.   Note on the Citation of Parliamentary Papers

(a)   *House and Command Papers*

(i)   *Form of Citation.* References to parliamentary papers should be accurate, adequate and simple. A great deal of unnecessary trouble has been given to readers even of scholarly works because the author's references do not meet these requirements. Yet it is an essentially straightforward matter if heed is paid to the simple scheme which Hansard put forward in his first *General Alphabetical Index, 1801–1826,* in the express hope that it would become standard practice; it has in fact remained the practice of the general alphabetical indexes.

The form he suggested for reference to a paper was:

session/paper no./volume no./volume page no.

If the title has not been given in the text, the form should be preceded by the title and description:

title and description/session/paper no./volume no./volume page no.

Examples:

Game Law. Sel. Cttee. Rep.; 1845 (602) xii, 331
London Squares. R.Com. Rep.; 1928–29 Cmd. 3196, viii, 111
London Squares. R.Com. mins. of ev.; 1927–28 Non-Parl.

An examination of the general alphabetical indexes will show that the semi-colon is invariably used to separate the descriptive part of the reference giving the title, etc., from the numerical part giving the session, paper and volume numbers and volume page numbers.

For a reference to a statement on a particular page of a paper, the title and description should be followed by the *printed* page number of the paper:

title, etc./printed page no./session/paper no./volume no./vol. page no.

Example:

Finance and Industry. Cttee. Rep. p. 134;
1930–31 Cmd.3897, xiii, 219.

All references should be made to the *House of Commons* bound sets, *except* where the paper is in the House of Lords set only. From this it follows:

a. Where the paper is the report of a Lords select committee (communicated to the Commons) it must be marked HL to indicate this and to distinguish it from a Commons select committee:

Sale of Beer. Sel. Cttee. HL. Rep; 1850 (398) xviii, 483.

b. Where the paper is in the Lords papers only, HL should be added to the paper number. This can be done either in the form HL (259) or (HL. 259):

title, etc./session/paper no./volume no./volume page no.

Example:

Despatch of Business. Sel. Cttee. HL. Rep. p. iv;
1867 (HL. 259) xxvii, 1.

For the reasons given below, the use of the volume page number is not strictly necessary, and may be regarded as optional.

These forms of citation are both adequate and simple, and are recommended as standard practice.

(ii) *Explanation*. The general form suggested by Hansard is self-explanatory, and only two 'rules' or 'conventions' need to be added to take account of the fact (1) that there are two sets of papers—the House of Commons papers and the House of Lords papers; (2) that in some 'official' bound sets, there are two paginations, a paper and a volume pagination, and (3) that two kinds of reference may be needed, one to identify a document and to show where it may be found, the other to indicate the page of an individual paper which contains a certain statement or figure.

(1) All references should be to the *House of Commons* sets of papers, except in those cases where the paper is found only in the Lords papers. The paper number should then be preceded by HL. There are three reasons for this rule. First, it was the practice of each House to communicate important papers to the other; such communicated House of Lords papers are thus included in the Commons set, with a Commons number. With certain exceptions Command papers are in the Commons set.[1] Collections of Lords papers are even scarcer than those of the Commons and are often of more meagre and sketchy character. The fullest sets are those of the British Museum, London School of Economics, the Bodleian, Cambridge University, Trinity College, Dublin and several government departments. For this reason not only are references to Lords papers not strictly necessary when the papers are already in the Commons set, but they are of use for work in the main scholastic libraries only if the imperfect collection should chance to have the particular paper. It is therefore unnecessary to encumber references by giving *both* House of Commons and House of Lords references, or by beginning each Commons reference by 'HC.' It is

1 K. A. C. Parsons, *A Checklist of British Parliamentary Papers (Bound Set), 1801–1950* (Cambridge 1958). See Appendixes I and II for the exceptions.

sufficient to use 'HL.' in those cases where the paper is in the Lords set only. The rule therefore greatly simplifies the form of reference.

(2) Page numbers. Each paper has its own printed page numbering, but the papers are in due course collected together, arranged in groups and bound in sessional sets. A certain number of copyright and 'official' sets are then given a continuous pagination for each volume. (a) All references to the text of an individual paper should use the *printed* page number of the paper. This has the advantage not only of following the table of contents of the paper and any page number used by the committee or author to refer to its own report, but meets the needs of readers who have access only to individual papers or to sets without volume pagination. (b) The volume page numbers are thus of use only for showing a reader where a paper is placed within a known volume. It is these volume page numbers which are given in the sessional and general alphabetical indexes, and they do assist a reader in finding a paper quickly in a set with such page numbers. Nevertheless, their use may perhaps be regarded as optional. They are of small value when the collections are without this pagination, or where, as occasionally happens, a volume has been privately given a manuscript numbering in imitation of the official one which is inaccurate. And of recent years, an increasing number of the quarto bound sets not bearing any volume pagination are being acquired by libraries. Each volume has a printed table of contents, which uses this numbering to show at what point in the volume the paper may be found. Session, paper number and volume alone will lead the reader to the right volume, and the table of contents will tell him the rest. It can therefore safely be omitted, and it is a matter of personal preference whether one provides the extra convenience of the volume page numbers.

(b) *Non-Parliamentary Papers*

These are best simply described as 'Non-Parl.' with the calendar year of issue and, where they are not the minutes of evidence of a royal commission, the name of the department issuing the paper. Formerly H.M.S.O. for its own purposes gave non-parliamentary papers over a certain low price a code number (replaced in 1968 by the Standard Book Number), and this may occasionally serve to distinguish two documents very similar in title. The SBN will always do so, and has the departments code number built in. There is an SBN index in the annual catalogue. The best form of reference is a precise statement of committee and document. its title and date of issue.

(c) *Titles*

Care may be needed in the citation of titles, especially those of nineteenth-century papers. See *Select List, 1833–1899*, pp. ix, x.

(d)   *Debates*

The official method of citation is as follows:
  volume no./House/series/date/column no.
Example:
  213 H.C. Deb. 5s. 8 Feb. 1928, col. 136.

Column numbers for written answers are always in italics.

II.   Arrangement of Unbound and Incomplete Collections

Difficulties are sometimes experienced in arranging unbound, incomplete collections of sessional papers, and this note on the methods of dealing with them has been prepared in response to a number of requests.

(a)   *Sessional Papers*

In general, the decisive means of identifying a paper are its session and House or Command number. From this it follows that any arrangement adopted should be such as can be used with the sessional and general alphabetical indexes and with footnote references based upon them. The reader should be able to pass directly from either of them to the paper and not be required to go through some intermediate process. The rule for guidance is that 'a paper out of numerical order is lost.' Readers requiring help on subjects can consult the Breviates and lists in section IV of this chapter which give the required numbers and sessions.

Unbound sessional papers can therefore be placed in box files in sessional and numerical order, the box files for bills, House papers and commands being arranged in that order for each session. This corresponds with the numerical list in the sessional indexes and H.M.S.O. Catalogue. The paper numbers of all papers in each box should be displayed on the spine of the box files. Searcher or librarian, as the case may be, can then go straight from the indexes or footnote references to the papers. This can be applied equally where the library acquires a selection of current parliamentary papers. If sessional indexes are not available for the nineteenth century, the order-to-print dates on the paper can be used to assign papers to their correct sessions. For sessional dates in the twentieth century, see Butler and Freeman, *British Political Facts,* and for Command numbers, *A Numerical Finding List of British Command Papers 1833-1961/62,* by E. di Roma and J. A. Rosenthal (New York Public Library 1967).

These arrangements are tidy and make for the effective use of indexes and footnote references. According to the circumstances, certain possible exceptions are suggested by experience. First, annual reports and statistical series, such as the reports of the Commissioners of Inland Revenue and the Statistical Abstracts, can be put separately in serial runs. Secondly, the papers of one or two very large Royal Commissions, such as those on the *Poor Laws* or *Labour,* if complete, may sometimes be conveniently put together; but such exceptions cannot be multiplied without destroying the simplicity of the whole system.

(b)   *Accession Lists*

In order to cope with an expanding collection of papers, complete sessional (numerical) lists of House paper numbers from 1801 and of Command numbers from 1833 can be made from information given on pages 23 and 25. As papers are added to the collection, either individually or in odd bound volumes, the list is ticked. In this way there is no problem of the list becoming obsolete, and identification is easy.

(c)   *Lords Papers*

(i)   *Communicated Commons Papers.* As many House of Commons papers were communicated to the Lords, any such paper can be added to a Commons collection by finding its Commons number in the general alphabetical indexes, placing it in its sessional numerical order and ticking the Commons number on the accession list. Odd bound volumes can be analysed in this way also.

(ii)   *Papers not Communicated to the Commons.* These can be made easily accessible if, after abstracting all the communicated documents, one arranges them in sessional-numerical order in box files and makes an accession list as for the Commons papers. In this way Lords papers are accessible from the indexes and all duplication with the Commons papers, which so increases their bulk, is avoided.

(d)   *Non-Parliamentary Papers*

Whether a library takes all non-parliamentary papers or selects according to the particular needs of the individual library, a fairly common practice in academic libraries is to file these papers by the year of publication and within the year by the department of origin to correspond with the H.M.S.O. catalogue. Each paper held can be ticked in the catalogue, and the H.M.S.O. card for each paper can provide an alphabetical index to the holdings.

III.   Dates of Parliamentary Sessions, 1801-1950

1801	22 Jan.–2 July 1801	1805	15 Jan.–12 July 1805
1801–02	29 Oct. 1801–28 June 1802	1806	21 Jan.–23 July 1806
		1806–07	15 Dec. 1806–27 Apr. 1807
1802–03	16 Nov. 1802–12 Aug. 1803	1807	22 June–14 Aug. 1807
1803–04	22 Nov. 1803–31 July 1804	1808	21 Jan.–4 July
		1809	19 Jan.–21 June 1809

1810	23 Jan.–21 June 1810		1844	1 Feb.–5 Sept. 1844
1810–11	1 Nov. 1810–24 July 1811		1845	4 Feb.–9 Aug. 1845
1812	7 Jan.–30 July 1812		1846	22 Jan.–28 Aug. 1846
1812–13	24 Nov. 1812–22 July 1813		1847	19 Jan.–23 July 1847
1813–14	4 Nov. 1813–30 July 1814		1847–48	18 Nov. 1847–5 Sept. 1848
1814–15	8 Nov. 1814–12 July 1815		1849	1 Feb.–1 Aug. 1849
1816	1 Feb.–2 July 1816		1850	31 Jan.–15 Aug. 1850
1817	28 Jan.–12 July 1817		1851	4 Feb.–8 Aug. 1851
1818	27 Jan.–10 June 1818		1852	3 Feb.–1 July 1852
1819	14 Jan.–13 July 1819		1852–53	4 Nov. 1852–20 Aug. 1853
1819–20	23 Nov. 1819–28 Feb. 1820		1854	31 Jan.–12 Aug. 1854
1820	21 Apr.–23 Nov. 1820		1854–55	12 Dec. 1854–14 Aug. 1855
1821	23 Jan.–11 July 1821		1856	31 Jan.–29 July 1856
1822	5 Feb.–6 Aug. 1822		1857 I	3 Feb.–21 Mar. 1857
1823	4 Feb.–19 July 1823		1857 II	30 Apr.–28 Aug. 1857
1824	3 Feb.–25 June 1824		1857–58	3 Dec. 1857–2 Aug. 1858
1825	3 Feb.–6 July 1825		1859 I	3 Feb.–19 Apr. 1859
1826	2 Feb.–31 May 1826		1859 II	31 May–13 Aug. 1859
1826–27	21 Nov. 1826–2 July 1827		1860	24 Jan.–28 Aug. 1860
1828	29 Jan.–28 July 1828		1861	5 Feb.–6 Aug. 1861
1829	5 Feb.–24 June 1829		1862	6 Feb.–7 Aug. 1862
1830	5 Feb.–23 July 1830		1863	5 Feb.–28 July 1863
1830–31	26 Oct. 1830–22 Apr. 1831		1864	4 Feb.–29 July 1864
1831–32	6 Dec. 1831–16 Aug. 1832		1865	7 Feb.–6 July 1865
1833	29 Jan.–29 Aug. 1833		1866	1 Feb.–10 Aug. 1866
1834	4 Feb.–15 Aug. 1834		1867	5 Feb.–21 Aug. 1867
1835	19 Feb.–10 Sept. 1835		1867–68	19 Nov. 1867–31 July 1868
1836	4 Feb.–20 Aug. 1836		1868–69	10 Dec. 1868–11 Aug. 1869
1837	31 Jan.–17 July 1837		1870	8 Feb.–10 Aug. 1870
1837–38	15 Nov. 1837–16 Aug. 1838		1871	9 Feb.–21 Aug. 1871
1839	5 Feb.–27 Aug. 1839		1872	6 Feb.–10 Aug. 1872
1840	16 Jan.–11 Aug. 1840		1873	6 Feb.–5 Aug. 1873
1841 I	26 Jan.–22 June 1841		1874	5 Mar.–7 Aug. 1874
1841 II	19 Aug.–7 Oct. 1841		1875	5 Feb.–13 Aug. 1875
1842	3 Feb.–12 Aug. 1842		1876	8 Feb.–15 Aug. 1876
1843	2 Feb.–24 Aug. 1843		1877	8 Feb.–14 Aug. 1877
			1878	17 Jan.–16 Aug. 1878
			1878–79	5 Dec. 1878–15 Aug. 1879

1880 I	5 Feb.–24 Mar. 1880	1914–16	11 Nov. 1914–27 Jan. 1916
1880 II	29 Apr.–7 Sept. 1880	1916	15 Feb.–22 Dec. 1916
1881	6 Jan.–27 Aug. 1881	1917–18	7 Feb. 1917–6 Feb. 1918
1882	7 Feb.–2 Dec. 1882		
1883	15 Feb.–25 Aug. 1883	1918	12 Feb.–21 Nov. 1918
1884	5 Feb.–14 Aug. 1884	1919	4 Feb.–23 Dec. 1919
1884–85	23 Oct. 1884–14 Aug. 1885	1920	10 Feb.–23 Dec. 1920
1886 I	12 Jan.–25 June 1886	1921 I	15 Feb.–10 Nov. 1921
1886 II	5 Aug.–25 Sept. 1886	1921 II	14 Dec.–19 Dec. 1921
1887	27 Jan.–16 Sept. 1887	1922 I	7 Feb.–4 Aug. 1922
1888	9 Feb.–24 Dec. 1888	1922 II	20 Nov.–15 Dec. 1922
1889	21 Feb.–30 Aug. 1889	1923	13 Feb.–16 Nov. 1923
1890	11 Feb.–18 Aug. 1890	1924	8 Jan.–9 Oct. 1924
1890–91	25 Nov. 1890–5 Aug. 1891	1924–25	2 Dec. 1924–22 Dec. 1925
1892 I	9 Feb.–28 June 1892	1926	2 Feb.–15 Dec. 1926
1892 II	4 Aug.–18 Aug. 1892	1927	8 Feb.–22 Dec. 1927
1893–94	31 Jan. 1893–5 Mar. 1894	1928	7 Feb.–3 Aug. 1928
1894	12 Mar.–25 Aug. 1894	1928–29	6 Nov. 1928–10 May 1929
1895 I	5 Feb.–6 July 1895	1929–30	25 June 1929–1 Aug. 1930
1895 II	12 Aug.–5 Sept. 1895		
1896	11 Feb.–14 Aug. 1896	1930–31	28 Oct. 1930–7 Oct. 1931
1897	19 Jan.–6 Aug. 1897		
1898	8 Feb.–12 Aug. 1898	1931–32	3 Nov. 1931–17 Nov. 1932
1899 I	7 Feb.–9 Aug. 1899		
1899 II	17 Oct.–27 Oct. 1899	1932–33	22 Nov. 1932–17 Nov. 1933
1900 I	30 Jan.–8 Aug. 1900		
1900 II	3 Dec.–15 Dec. 1900	1933–34	21 Nov. 1933–16 Nov. 1934
1901	23 Jan.–17 Aug. 1901		
1902	16 Jan.–18 Dec. 1902	1934–35	20 Nov. 1934–25 Oct. 1935
1903	17 Feb.–14 Aug. 1903		
1904	2 Feb.–15 Aug. 1904	1935–36	26 Nov. 1935–30 Oct. 1936
1905	14 Feb.–11 Aug. 1905		
1906	13 Feb.–21 Dec. 1906	1936–37	3 Nov. 1936–22 Oct. 1937
1907	12 Feb.–28 Aug. 1907		
1908	29 Jan.–21 Dec. 1908	1937–38	26 Oct. 1937–4 Nov. 1938
1909	16 Feb.–3 Dec. 1909		
1910	15 Feb.–28 Nov. 1910	1938–39	8 Nov. 1938–23 Nov. 1939
1911	31 Jan.–16 Dec. 1911		
1912–13	14 Feb. 1912–7 Mar. 1913	1939–40	28 Nov. 1939–20 Nov. 1940
1913	10 Mar.–15 Aug. 1913	1940–41	21 Nov. 1940–11 Nov. 1941
1914	10 Feb.–18 Sept. 1914		

1941–42	12 Nov. 1941–10 Nov. 1942	1946–47	12 Nov. 1946–20 Oct. 1947
1942–43	11 Nov. 1942–23 Nov. 1943	1947–48	21 Oct. 1947–13 Sept. 1948
1943–44	24 Nov. 1943–28 Nov. 1944	1948	14 Sept.–25 Oct. 1948
1944–45	29 Nov. 1944–15 June 1945	1948–49	26 Oct. 1948–16 Dec. 1949
1945–46	1 Aug. 1945–6 Nov. 1946	1950	1 Mar. 1950–26 Oct. 1950

IV. Lists, Breviates, Guides, etc.

Adam, M. I., Ewing, J., and Munro, J. *Guide to the Principal Parliamentary Papers Relating to the Dominions, 1812–1911.* Edinburgh: Oliver & Boyd, 1913.

Bond, M. F. *The Records of Parliament: A Guide for Genealogists and Local Historians.* Canterbury: Phillimore, 1964.

Di Roma, E., and Rosenthal, J. A., comps. *A Numerical Finding List of British Command Papers Published 1833–1961/62.* New York: N.Y. Public Library, 1967.

Ford, P., and Ford, G. *A Breviate of Parliamentary Papers, 1900–1916* (volume I). Oxford, 1957. Reprinted Shannon: Irish Univ. Press, 1969.

——. *A Breviate of Parliamentary Papers, 1917–1939* (volume II). Oxford, 1951. Reprinted Shannon: Irish Univ. Press, 1969.

——. *A Breviate of Parliamentary Papers, 1940–1954* (volume III). Oxford: Blackwell, 1961.

——. *Select List of British Parliamentary Papers, 1833–1899.* Oxford, 1953. Reprinted Shannon: Irish Univ. Press, 1970.

Ford, P.; Ford, G., and Marshallsay, Diana. *Select List of British Parliamentary Papers, 1955–1964.* Shannon: Irish Univ. Press, 1970.

Hansard, Luke G. *Catalogue of Parliamentary Reports and a Breviate of Their Contents, 1696–1834.* Reprinted with introduction by P. and G. Ford. Shannon: Irish Univ. Press, 1969.

Jones, H. V., comp. *Catalogue of Parliamentary Papers, 1801–1900, with a Few of Earlier Date* (King's List). London: P. S. King and Son, 1904.

——. *Catalogue of Parliamentary Papers, 1901–10.* London: P. S. King and Son, 1912.

——. *Catalogue of Parliamentary Papers, 1911–1920.* London: P. S. King and Son, 1922.

[These volumes are of limited use; they have no official reference numbers.]

Lambert, Sheila. *Bills and Acts: Legislative Procedure in Eighteenth Century England.* Cambridge: Cambridge University Press, 1971.

——, ed. *List of House of Commons Sessional Papers, 1701–1750.* London: List and Index, 1968.

Morgan, A. M., ed. *British Government Publications: An Index to Chairmen and Authors, 1941–1966.* London: Library Association, 1969.

Ollé, J. G. *An Introduction to British Government Publications.* London: Association of Assistant Librarians, 1965.

Parsons, K. A. C. *A Checklist of the British Parliamentary Papers (Bound Set), 1801–1950.* Cambridge: University Library, 1958.

Pemberton, J. E. *British Official Publications.* Oxford: Pergamon Press, 1971.

Powell, W. R. *Local History from Blue Books.* London: Historical Association, 1962.

Temperley, Harold W. V., and Penson, Lillian M. *A Century of Diplomatic Blue Books, 1814–1914.* Cambridge: Cambridge Univ. Press, 1938.

Vogel, R. *A Breviate of British Diplomatic Blue Books, 1919–1939.* Montreal: McGill Univ. Press, 1963.

V. Official Guides to Sources, Indexes and Publications

Bond, M. F. *Guide to the Records of Parliament.* H.M.S.O., 1971.

House of Lords Record Office Memoranda (duplicated typescript):
13. The Journals, Minutes and Committee Books of the House of Lords
16. The Private Bill Records of the House of Lords
18. A Guide to Parliament Office Papers
20. A Guide to House of Lords Papers and Petitions

House of Commons Library Documents (published by H.M.S.O.):
1. Acts of Parliament: Some Distinctions in their Nature and Numbering. 1955.
2. A Bibliography of Parliamentary Debates of Great Britain. 1956.
5. Access to Subordinate Legislation. 1963.
7. The Journal of the House of Commons. 1971.
8. Votes and Standing Orders of the House of Commons: The Beginning. 1971.

Guides to Official Sources. Non. Parl. General Register Office:
1. Labour Statistics; 1950. Rev. ed.; 1958
2. Census Reports of Great Britain, 1801–1931; 1951
3. Local Government Statistics; 1953
4. Agricultural and Food Statistics; 1958

5. Social Security Statistics; 1961
6. Census of Production Reports; 1961

Studies in Official Statistics. Non. Parl. Central Statistical Office:
11. List of Principal Statistical Series Available. I. Economic Statistics. II. Financial Statistics. III. Regional Statistics; 1965
13. National Accounts Statistics. Sources and Methods, ed. by R. Maurice; 1968
14. Agricultural and Food Statistics. A Guide to Official Sources: 1969.

National Economic Development Office. *Distributive Trades Statistics: A Guide to Official Sources.* H.M.S.O., 1970

National Economic Development Office. *Motor Industry Statistics 1960–1969.* N.E.D.O., 1971.

Government Publications. Official Indexes, Lists, Guides and Catalogues. H.M.S.O., 1956.

H.M. Treasury. *Official Publications.* H.M.S.O., 1958.

Published by H.M.S.O. A Brief Guide to Official Publications. H.M.S.O., 1960.

British Museum State Paper Room. *Check List of British Official Serial Publications.* 5th ed. to June 1971. State Paper Room, 1971 (annual duplicated typescript).

Guide to Government Department and other Libraries and Information Bureaux. 19th ed. London: Ministry of Defence, 1969.

Sectional Lists of Government Publications. H.M.S.O.

INDEX